Raymon
January

THE SCIENCE OF FLY-FISHING

THE
SCIENCE
OF
Fly-Fishing

STAN L. ULANSKI

UNIVERSITY OF VIRGINIA PRESS
CHARLOTTESVILLE AND LONDON

University of Virginia Press

© 2003 by the Rector and Visitors of the University of Virginia

Figures 1 and 22–27 ©2003 by Adrienne Gruver

9 8 7 6 5 4 3 2 1

LIBRARY OF CONGRESS CATALOGING-IN-PUBLICATION DATA
Ulanski, Stan L., 1946–
    The science of fly-fishing / Stan L. Ulanski.
        p.   cm.
Includes bibliographical references and index.
        ISBN 0-8139-2210-0 (cloth : alk. paper)
    1. Fly fishing. I. Title.
    SH456 .U43 2003
    799.1'24—dc21

                                        2003006713

Contents

Illustrations

TABLES

Preface

AS REFLECTED IN THE VOLUMINOUS PUBLICATION
record of fly-fishing articles and books, the sport of fly-fishing
occupies a position of unique importance in our culture and
society. Though fly-fishing requires a nearly scientific level of
knowledge on the part of the participant, there is, at present,
no work that integrates the many scientific components of the
aquatic realm into the activity of fly-fishing. My intent in
writing this book is to establish the robust link between fly-
fishing and the science that permeates the evolution of this angling technique. It is hoped that my approach will allow the
reader to achieve a level of understanding presently not at-
tainable from the extant fly-fishing literature. It is my opinion that a deeper understanding of the science of fly-fishing
will only make those angling experiences richer.

The foundations of fly-fishing history and literature are
firmly rooted in the disciplines of science. Any successful fly
angler is indebted to the endeavors of entomologists, fisheries
biologists, rod developers, and aquatic geochemists, to name
a few. This book attempts to describe the scientific components that are intrinsic to fly-fishing. One goal of the book is
to present the essential elements of the physical and biological sciences in a manner that will enable the reader to see their
practical application to the environment and the recreational
activity of fly-fishing. The abundance and vitality of aquatic
life in a stream or lake are intrinsically linked to the seasonal
cycle of change, be these changes in temperature, water flow,
or nutrients. For example, though many fly anglers intuitively
recognize the importance of water temperature in locating fish

within a stream, they may be hard-pressed to elucidate the reasons for species dependence upon temperature. This book will couch the temperature tolerance of certain aquatic organisms in terms of their evolutionary lineage, the temperature dependence of a species' prey, and their innate instinct to reproduce. Though there are many books on *how to* fish, that is not the purpose of this book but rather that the reader will attain a level of understanding of the natural settings and physical requirements of the fish being pursued. Many of these aquatic environments are of considerable beauty and grace, and that in itself should warrant their study and our concern for their preservation. Just as fishing, by its very nature, is an interrogatory pursuit, this book will attempt to provide the incentive for the angler to investigate fully the nuances and subtleties intrinsic to fly-fishing.

The Science of Fly-Fishing is written for those anglers who want to take the "next step" in understanding their sport. Though most anglers can grasp the technical aspects of their sport (casting methodology, fly selection), this book will appeal to those readers who want to comprehend the physical principles associated with a good cast or why polarized sunglasses allow the angler to spot that trophy trout beneath the water surface. The reader that I have in mind is the "fly-fishing aficionado-student of the sport." Though the scientific concepts as they relate to fly-fishing are developed systematically, logically, and rigorously, their comprehension requires no more than a good dose of common sense and a rudimentary knowledge of basic scientific principles. The book was designed for those anglers who are curious about the relevance of science to fly-fishing but have little formal background in science. In some chapters, for the more quantitatively oriented reader, I have included Technical Focus sections that expand on the material in the text or explore a subject closely related to what is being discussed.

I have tended to confine my discussions to the salmonids, mainly trout and salmon, and their freshwater environment. This exclusiveness is not to be taken as a slight on other freshwater species (bass, pike, panfish) but in part reflects the broad appeal of the salmonids among anglers and their place in the history of angling literature. However, much of what I have written about the physical, chemical, and biological environment of salmonids is applicable to other species.

Will reading this book make you a better fly angler? While there are many elements in this book that have direct applicability to angling situations, the main thrust of this book is to set the foundation for continued inquiry and lifelong pursuit into the activity of fly-fishing. With this declaration, I invite you to deepen your understanding of the scientific nature of fly-fishing, which will hopefully improve your appreciation of the salmonid and add to the quality of the angling moment. If at the end of this book you have embraced the sentiment that the fly angler's search is for more than just fish, then my effort in writing this book will have been rewarded.

Acknowledgments

I WOULD ESPECIALLY LIKE TO RECOGNIZE THE students of my "Fly-Fishing and Environment" class, who, as a collective group, were exposed to early drafts of the manuscript. Their comments regarding the nature, difficulty, and structuring of the material significantly improved the final product.

A special thanks to my wife, Linda Ulanski, who critically reviewed the manuscript and aptly aided in the drafting of the figures.

Every author, myself included, is indebted to the anonymous reviewers who give of their time to carefully critique a manuscript and offer valuable suggestions for its overall improvement. I truly value their contribution to the publication process. Finally, I would like to express my appreciation to Ms. Boyd Zenner, Acquisitions Editor at the University of Virginia Press, who was the first to express a sincere interest in my project.

THE SCIENCE OF FLY-FISHING

The Mystique and History of Fly-Fishing: Angling through the Ages

THE SPORT OF FLY-FISHING HAS OFTEN BEEN EM-bellished in hyperbole. Fly anglers have frequently thought of this activity as being the only "pure" way to catch fish and consequently looked down upon the bait fishermen. William Trotter Porter, writing in the *Turf Register* in the 1830s, put it this way: "Fly fishing has been designated the royal and aristocratic branch of the angler's art . . . the most difficult, the most elegant, and to men of taste, by myriad of degrees the most exciting and most pleasing mode of angling." Part of this snobbery can be attributed to the social structure in Britain during the nineteenth century. In Britain, class division is quite evident in fishing. Mark Browning, writing in *Haunted by Waters: Fly Fishing in North America* (1998), postulates that fishing in Britain is inextricably tied to the land and specifically to the ownership of the land. Fish are viewed as personal property—with the salmon on one plane and the lowly pike relegated to a reduced status. However, we are jumping ahead of the story on the evolution of fly-fishing throughout history. Let's begin our journey with the earliest anglers who long ago set the stage for modern fly-fishing.

Although Izaak Walton (1593–1683) is generally credited for introducing the art of angling to the modern world, this activity was practiced throughout antiquity. As pointed out by R. W. Dunfield in *The Atlantic Salmon in the History of North America* (1985), the word *angle,* in its original meaning, did not imply the use of a rod but meant simply to fish with a hook or angle. Dating back to biblical periods, there are references to angling: "They take up all of them [fish] with the angle, they catch them in their net, and gather them in their drag: Therefore they rejoice and are glad" (Habakkuk 1:15).

We know from archeological findings that the first fish hooks were invented about twenty thousand years ago in the south of Europe. These forerunners of the modern hook are probably the *gorges*—slender pieces of bone or wood with a groove in the middle for attaching a line (McDonald 1954). The hooks were fastened on a line made of animal sinews or from thin, tough plant material such as roots or vines. Using worms, mussels, or other natural food sources for bait, these Stone Age people were the first to try their luck in the art of angling.

By the year 5000 BC, angling was becoming relatively sophisticated. Archaeological finds have included floats that were cut from bark and used in conjunction with hooks for fishing. Three thousand years later, Egyptian paintings were the first to portray the equivalent of present-day angling. These paintings showed how to fish with a rod, a line tied directly to the tip of the rod, and a hook. These barbless hooks were generally made of copper and were bent into a shape similar to a youngster's pin hook. Even Cleopatra dabbled in the art of angling, but with the unorthodox approach of having divers impale a fish on her hook to guarantee her success. (Royalty does have its perquisites.) The first fly angler was probably also Egyptian as evidenced by a 1400 BC temple drawing showing a man holding a short rod to which is affixed seven individual lines, each with a flying insect. The next evolutionary step occurred about 200 BC when the Chinese began using metal hooks with barbs and silk lines. Until around the beginning of the 1960s, most fly lines were made of silk.

The first printed material about fly-fishing is in the book *De natura animalium,* written in the year 20 AD by the Greek Claudius Aeliannus. He relates that the Macedonians, fishing on the Astreus River, invented the fly. They tied red wool and cock feathers to a hook to imitate a buzzing insect favored by brown trout. The Macedonian fishermen dangled their flies at the length of 6-foot lines affixed to sticks of equal length (Herd 2001).

By the Middle Ages, the first report describing fly-fishing as a sport was published. In the year 1496, the article "A Treatyse of Fyshynge Wyth an Angle" was published in *Book of St. Albans*. It described a 20-foot fishing pole with iron hoops, horsehair line, and the use of several types of feather-dressed hooks—flies. In particular, there are precise instructions on the construction of the twisted horsehair line and the type of hair to use in the process. Though there is some debate about the authorship, the work is generally attributed to Dame Juliana Berners. She described for the first time how trout and salmon were caught by means of artificial flies. Probably, being an amateur aquatic entomologist, Dame Berners discovered the seasonal cycle of various insects. She noted that fish varied their diet depending upon what insect hatches were available on the stream. In this work, the angler was viewed as more than a hunter of fish, but also as an astute observer of nature, a philosopher, and an idealist. This "treatise" set the tone for future publications on fly-fishing. Unfortunately, there were no major publications on fly-fishing for another two centuries, when the seventeenth century ushered in a proliferation of angling literature.

During this period, anglers witnessed the publication of the *Art of Angling* (1651) by Thomas Barker, *The Compleat Angler* (1653) by Izaak Walton, and *The Experienc'd Angler* (1662) by Robert Venables. Of these writers, fly-angling historians consider Walton to have done the most to promote the sport from a social and moral aspect. His passion for the sport is in evidence when he wrote: "God never did make a more calm, quiet, innocent recreation" (1975, 22). But Walton's work also aroused considerable interest with its emphasis on equipment. The typical seventeenth-century angler employed horsehair line that was attached to homemade rods constructed of relatively light hazel wood. The skilled fishermen of Walton's time fished for trout with lines that tapered to three or four hairs, and experts fished with lines as light as one hair. Fighting a big trout became somewhat of a challenge, since the breaking strength on one hair is about four pounds. In some cases fly anglers utilized a simple reel attached to the butt of the rod. By 1655, Charles Kirby of England developed an improved hook that became the prototype for some hooks used today. By the end of the eighteenth century, multipiece rods with guides, line, and reel became commonplace in angling society.

The central theme of the English literature that was to follow Walton's publication was diametrically opposite to that of Walton. These authors considered fishing a battle with nature and jettisoned anything to do with introspection and connecting with nature.

Paul Taylor, a noted modern-day environmental ethicist, argues that this behavior demonstrates a lack of respect for nature because much of the enjoyment and challenge of fishing involves an attempt to deceive wild animals. As in the case of any deception, the deceiver assumes an elevated position in relation to the deceived. The deceived, the fish, is perceived to have a lower worth than the angler. It is interesting to note that one of the most common flies employed in modern fly-fishing is called a *deceiver*. It is not surprising, then, that by the middle of the 1700s many of the fly-angling practitioners were from the British military ranks. It was almost a requirement that an officer candidate in the British army demonstrate considerable skill in the art of angling. As the British influence spread around the globe, it was mainly the military that perpetuated fly-fishing in even uncivilized places like the American colonies. A true eighteenth-century gentlemen could maintain some sense of dignity by fly-angling for salmon in the virgin rivers of North America. Not to be outdone by the army, the British navy had its own fly-fishing devotee in none other than Lord Nelson. It was reported that his greatest regret after losing his arm in the battle of Tenerife in 1797 was that "we're spoilt for fly fishing" (Russel 1864, 28).

By the mid-1840s, though fly-fishing had relatively few hard-core advocates, Charles Hallock, a prominent fly angler of his time, reported that this activity was not widely practiced by the common folk in Britain. Their numbers were limited by the one overriding factor in pursuing any recreational activity—leisure time. During this period, free time was not a commodity that was available to most working Britons; therefore, angling was not practiced by the masses and thus became the sole domain of those with wealth and social status. For those privileged few capable of enjoying this activity, Scotland became the place to be trained and to perfect your fly-fishing skills, particularly for salmon, on the Tweed, Tay, Thorso, and a score of other prime Scottish rivers. Clubs were formed whose members had to abide by strict angling rules, codes of conduct, and rigid procedures. Like rising through the military ranks, club members rose in status and esteem in accordance with their angling skills. In Scotland, the unwritten edict was that a man was not a man until he had angled for a salmon. By the beginning of the twentieth century, there is little doubt that the cradle of modern fly-fishing and its associated literature was in England. English writers placed an emphasis on developing and using artificial patterns that imitated insects composing the diet of trout. Fishing dry flies on privately owned chalk streams became the province of a privileged few in British society. But in later years there is a marked shift in the output of fly-fishing literature to across the Atlantic.

Preceding modern literature is the influence of Native Americans on fishing lore. The material that makes its way into the literature often comes about through a circuitous route and is not obvious. In contrast to the European tradition of viewing the fish as an adversary to be overcome by cunning and skill, the Native Americans developed a more personal relationship with the fish they depended upon for sustenance. In his book *The Year of the Trout* (1995), Steve Raymond writes that salmon and steelhead took on a mystical, even religious significance to the tribes of the Pacific Northwest. Because of their reverence for these fish, the local Native Americans were probably the first to develop angling ethics. They never took more, no matter how plentiful the salmon runs, than they needed. Since their regimen of life was tied to a subsistence economy based upon a nomadic existence, it was not in the culture of the Native Americans to store up great quantities of food.

This approach was in sharp contrast, for the most part, to early Western philosophical tradition that denies any moral relationship exists between humans and nature. The main tenet of this tradition is that only human beings have moral standing; all other things have value only in that they serve human interests. The two philosophers most associated with this tradition, Aristotle and Thomas Aquinas, proposed views that showed little interest in assigning moral status to forms of life other than human. Aristotle writes, "All other animals exist for the sake of man, tame animals for use he can make of them as well as for the food they provide; and as for wild animals, most though not all can be used for food" (1941, 1256). Sixteen centuries later, Thomas Aquinas picks up on this theme but expresses it in a more theological context: "We refute the error of those who claim that it is sin for man to kill brute animals. For animals are ordered to man in the natural course of things, according to divine providence. Consequently, man uses them without any injustice, either by killing them or employing them in any other way" (1924, 435).

Though probably not known for his fly-fishing prowess, Henry David Thoreau, through his writings about nature, employs the sport of fishing as an active metaphor for religion and the spiritual life. To Thoreau, fishing was a religious experience—primacy of the spiritual over the material. One's life should be spent in earnest contemplation of one's natural surroundings and its inhabitants. Thoreau's attempt to mix in his writings the contemplative aspect of the mind with the active pursuit of fish is an approach that was essentially foreign to English writers. This kinship of fly-fishing to religion in spiritual intensity and dogma prevails even today. Who doesn't know a fly-fishing aficionado that takes almost a liturgical approach to the sport? (The *only* way to approach a trout is an upstream quartering cast.) On the flip side of the coin, many religious zealots among the American colonists viewed angling as a sinful pursuit—its allure seemingly the strongest on Sundays and other religious holidays. They questioned angling on the moral ground that it inflicted undue pain on one of God's creatures. (This is an argument similar to one now proposed by People for the Ethical Treatment of Animals [PETA] to ban fishing.) Debate raged even among the clergy with regard to the sinfulness of angling. Cotton Mather in 1721 went on record in chastising certain preachers of the Gospel for idling away their time angling. But the Reverend Secomb in 1739 proclaimed that angling was sinless in the sight of God. I guess the expression "cast away sin" was open to interpretation during this period.

Apart from this religious aspect, many of the industrious colonists considered fly-fishing a waste of time and money. Imbued with the Protestant work ethic, many settlers considered it inconceivable that anyone would expend the effort and resources to catch a few fish by angling in lieu of catching many fish by net. They couldn't comprehend why anyone would want to tramp though dense woods and undergrowth, ward off hordes of bloodsucking insects, and wade cold, swift streams to cast a line to some undersized trout. This Puritan opinion of wilderness is not surprising, since they viewed the wilderness as an area to be avoided and feared. The wilderness was an area abandoned by God and home to the devil. Using the writings of the Old Testament, Puritans preached that the wilderness was a barren and desolate place. Even the Bible states that Adam and Eve were banished from the Garden of Eden into an "accursed" wilderness.

In contrast to this Puritan outlook, another model emerged that viewed the wilderness as a symbol of innocence and purity. Joseph Des Jardins refers to this paradigm as the romantic model; the wilderness is the last remaining area of unspoiled and uncorrupted nature. In this model wilderness is identified with Paradise, the Garden of Eden. While fly anglers of today would probably support this view of wilderness, the philosophical underpinnings of this model can be found in the writings of Ralph Waldo Emerson and Henry David Thoreau. They argued that true understanding comes only when we grasp a deeper or "transcendent" reality—a reality unencumbered by human beliefs and values. Unspoiled by the corrupting influence of civilization, the wilderness is the most genuine example of transcendent reality. It allows humans to attain their closest contact with higher truths and beliefs. Similar to Thoreau retreating to his cabin on Walden Pond, the wilderness represents a retreat and respite from the pressures of society.

By the mid-nineteenth century, public attitudes about fly-fishing assumed a more positive slant, as evidenced by increased participation in the sport. This surge in popularity was brought about mainly by angling books—such as *Days and Nights of Salmon Fishing* (1843) by William Scrope, *An Angler in Canada, Nova Scotia and the United States* (1848) by Charles Lanman, and *Sporting Adventures in the New World* (1855) by Campbell Hardy—that extolled the pleasures of pursuing magnificent creatures in beautiful settings. These authors helped to dispel the notion that fly-fishing was simply a groveling activity pursued by the unkempt. The virtues of fly-fishing and its advocates became elevated and were extolled in the literature. While this "sea change" in attitude was certainly welcomed by the nineteenth-century practitioners of fly-fishing, it may have contributed to the opinion by some in the following century that fly-fishing is an elitist activity.

As we now approach the modern period in fly-fishing, one of the twentieth century's literary giants of fly-fishing is Roderick Haig-Brown (1908–1976). Although born in England, he lived most of his adult life in North America, and his writings reflect both schools of thought about fly-fishing. He did not see any conflict between the active and passive aspects of fishing. Haig-Brown acknowledges that, stripped to its bare essential, fishing is a sport—comprising the pursuit and catching of one's quarry. But his works reflect the repeated theme that fishing also involves a journey of self-discovery. This thread of introspection and finding meaning in one's life through angling continues to the present with such works as *Fly Fishing through Midlife Crisis* (1994) by Howell Raines and *Fly Fishing: A Life in Mid-Stream* (1996) by Turhan Tirana. In *Fisherman's Spring* (1975), Haig-Brown postulates that, while the technical aspects of fly-fishing are approaching their pinnacle, the experience of fly-fishing is still open to infinite creative interpretation.

While Haig-Brown did not earn his reputation on the strength of his angling expertise, Hemingway's fame is partially attributed to his macho approach to both hunting and fishing. As Browning writes, "For Hemingway fishing—fly and otherwise—was an important component in the mythos that he forged for himself; however, despite the legendary qualities of the author's life or his pastimes, it cannot be denied that fishing held a special place in the private man as well" (1998, 84). Hemingway actively incorporated his experiences into his works of fiction. He does this at times so convincingly that these fictional exploits and locations are often mistaken for Hemingway's own personal adventures. As pointed out by Lea Lawrence in *Prowling Papa's Waters: A Hemingway Odyssey* (1992), Hemingway's literary life was bracketed by angling stories: "Big Two-Hearted River" (1942), his first literary acclaimed work, and *The Old Man and the Sea* (1951), his last major work, for which he won the Nobel Prize.

One of the most intriguing questions posed in twentieth-century fly-fishing literature is, Why do we fish? To some authors the answer is relatively simple and uncomplicated: Anglers have to catch fish. Paul Quinnett expresses this feeling quite succinctly: "What you find at the very core of angling is the thrill of getting hold of a wild thing" (1994, 44). Theodore Gordon, father of American dry-fly-fishing, describes his best day of fishing solely in terms of catch. His goal is to quantify his experience to the reader.

Other writers have embraced the phrase *piscator non solum piscatur*—there is more to fishing than catching fish. We again turn to Thoreau, who best epitomizes this philosophy when he writes, "A man can spend his whole life in a stream without ever realizing it was not the trout he was after" (1997, 145). To some authors, the experience of fly-fishing assumes a religious significance. Bryn Hammond in *Halcyon Days: The Nature of Trout Fishing and Fishermen* (1994) notes the propensity for angling writers to reach for the divine. Mark Browning refers to this as "divine posturing." Norman Maclean, in *A River Runs through It*, adopts this attitude in the classic statement: "In our family, there was no clear line between fly fishing and religion" (1976, 1). Ted Leeson views the act of fly-fishing as a metaphysical experience, reaching a higher spiritual plane. He articulates this feeling when he writes, "The presence of a beautiful fish on a beautiful body of water is something so extraordinary as to provide an absolute bearing for the angler's moral compass" (1994, 117). Even President Herbert Hoover was prone to expressing his feelings regarding the spiritual aspect of fly-fishing: "Next to prayer, fishing is the most personal relationship of man" (1963, 76); and "Fishing is a chance to wash one's soul with pure air, with the rush of the brook, or the shimmer of the sun on blue water" (1963, 11).

Many writers have attempted to bridge the gulf between the sacred and secular poles of fly-fishing. The reason for fishing is not to find fish but to find oneself—a means to self-discovery and awareness. Similar to Zen meditation, fly-fishing is the medium to probe one's inner self. Teddy Roosevelt, though not an avid fly angler, refers to his outdoor adventures in terms of "drawing humans into the wilderness and drawing out the best from humans" (1998, 204). Bliss Perry in his writings assumes a slightly different posture: "Fishing in general has always seemed to me a form of subversion anyway. In a world that insists upon 'means' and 'ends,' that dooms every path to a destination, fishing eludes the categories and so slips the distinction altogether. You become engaged in the nonterminal, participial indefiniteness of 'going fishing.' To go fishing is essentially functionless though that's not at all the same as saying it is without purpose" (1927, 28). Mark Browning offers another perspective: "Fishing is, by its very nature, an uncertain and interrogatory endeavor. As in writing, painting, or any of a hundred other pursuits—the angler moves out of the realm of the known and into a creative realm of questions" (1998, 124). Nick Lyons, in attempting to answer a colleague's questioning why he must fish in order to enjoy the river, eloquently responds: "That shadow that I am pursuing beneath the amber water is hieroglyphic. I read its position, watch its relationship to a thousand other shadows. That shadow is a great glyph, connected to the swallow overhead, to the cream caddisfly, to the little cased larva on the stream bed, to the contours of the river; the velocity of the flow, the chemical composition and temperature of the water—and a thousand other factors. Fishing makes me a student of life" (1977, 15).

But why has fly-fishing, as compared to other forms of angling, dominated the fishing literature in terms of sheer volume of published material? Ted Leeson probably best articulates the appeal of fly-fishing: "Despite its reliance on the line, fly-fishing is not linear. It is radial and web-like. At the center is a rising trout, and millimeters above its nose is the fly. From it, paths trace outward to the engineering and art of tackle making, to geology and hydrology, botany and birds, aquatic and terrestrial insects, books, history, photography and a thousand other filaments" (1994, 49).

But there was a period immediately after World War II when fly-fishing was mired in a battle for converts to and practitioners of the sport. The period between 1945 and 1955 ushered in the advent of the spinning reel, which made it affordable and easy for novices to fish. Die-hard fly-fishing writers during this period fanned the flames of rivalry between fly anglers and spin fishers. Though it is debatable whether the spin-fishing phenomenon decreased the number of recruits to fly-fishing, it did not diminish the intellectual curiosity, devotion, and productivity of its most strident advocates. An icon of American fly-fishing (Schullery 1987) during this period was Lee Wulff, who was a major proponent of the use of Native American material in fly-tying and revolutionized salmon fishing with the adoption of the short rod. The literary standard-bearer during this period was Preston Jennings's *A Book of Trout Flies* (1935), which was expanded on over a period of time by wide-ranging anglers, searching and researching new streams and rivers. This entomological wave of creativity peaked with the 1955 publication of Ernest Schwiebert's *Matching the Hatch,* which emphasized selectivity in a fish's dietary habits and how anglers can counteract this apparent advantage. The next fifteen years was a relatively quiescent period in fly-fishing literature. Opinions abound attempting to explain this decrease in productivity. But one thing is certain: since the 1970s, fly-fishing popularity and its literary proponents have increased markedly. The proliferation of books, magazines, and even web sites that have been made available to the public have covered a broad spectrum of topics, including how-to articles on fishing the fly, casting, fly-tying, locating prime fishing destinations, and targeting specific species, to name a few. But I believe there is a whole genre of books that have attempted to demystify fly-fishing by taking a humorous approach to the sport. Books such as *Sex, Death and Fly-Fishing* (1990) by John Gierach and *Fishing Came First* (1989) by John Cole have shown that fly-fishing can be fun and rewarding in spite of our foibles if we make the effort to master this sport. Not to be outdone, the movie industry has also been responsible for the growth spurt in fly-fishing popularity as evidenced by the success of Robert Redford's movie portrayal of Maclean's novel *A River Runs through It*. Since its release, this movie and subsequent readings of Maclean's book have generated considerable interest about the moral undertones of the story. There is a scene in the movie when the brothers, Norman and Paul, are coerced into taking a novice angler fishing. Paul haughtily offers his opinion that their angling companion will probably bring along a coffee can of worms to fish for trout. Is Paul making a character judgment based on his perceived code of fly-fishing ethics? Certainly, many fly anglers would argue that ethical behavior is an important aspect of the sport of fly-fishing. Probably starting with the *Treatise*, Dame Berners devotes the concluding segments of the book to the question of the ethical qualities found in the "perfect" angler (VonKienbusch 1958). This theme of ethical behavior and angling etiquette is a constant message throughout Walton's work and continues today in the fly-angling literature.

In this same vein, many writers, philosophers, and naturalists have linked together the science of the natural world with an ethical perspective. Aldo Leopold (1887–1948) was an avid angler and perhaps the leading environmentalist of the twentieth century. Recognizing the problems associated with the land and wildlife practices of his day, he eventually developed the notion that land should be put aside for its recreational and aesthetic value alone. In times of spiraling human impact on the environment and acrimonious debates regarding resource allocation, there is an old adage that is particularly relevant today: "Science without ethics is blind; ethics without science is empty." The word *ethics* is derived from the Greek word *ethos,* literally meaning "custom." In this sense, ethics is a system of moral principles or values that guide customary behavior in a particular society, organization, or club. The community of fly anglers generally recognizes some customary rules of behavior that define the relationship among anglers. For example, the following ethical guidelines are a representative, but not inclusive list: (1) An angler working upstream has the right-of-way over someone fishing downstream; (2) Always yield to the angler with the fish on the line; (3) A section of water belongs to the first person fishing it; (4) A slow-moving or stationary angler has the right to remain in his current position without interruption.

But many fly anglers and organizations like Trout Unlimited and Federation of Fly Fishers have adopted a wider view of ethics than solely the responsibilities that we owe to other humans. This broader approach manifests itself in the discipline of environmental ethics. This ethical branch details the moral relations between humans and their natural environment. Environmental ethics attempt to enumerate what responsibilities humans have toward the natural world and to demonstrate how these responsibilities are justified. In this realm, fly anglers have assumed responsibility in managing endangered fisheries, reconstructing essential trout habitat, and supporting waterway cleanup projects. By making judgments, giving professional advice, and offering opinions on the pros and cons of certain endeavors, fly anglers assume the responsibility of prescribing behavior: "Dams should not be constructed on salmon runs." "Endangered fish species ought to receive our protection." "Water should not be withdrawn from trout rivers for agricultural purposes." This responsibility implicitly or explicitly warrants some standards of ethical behavior from those who have made the judgments and evaluations.

Though Michigan fly anglers instituted the practice of catch-and-release during the 1950s as a means of reducing the practice and expense of trout stream stocking, its current acceptance depends on the view of the human community in which the fishery resides. Part of the problem may be one of semantics. As Lyman (1999) points out, while the term *selective harvesting* may be acceptable to native Alaskans in rural areas, the phrase *catch-and-release* evokes a negative response and is interpreted as "playing with one's food." In British Columbia, where fish are a key component of their diet, the term *nonretention* appears less threatening. Wherever fish are an integral part of a society, the term *catch-and-release* must overcome a number of cultural taboos to be accepted. The fly-angling community has seized upon a number of opportunities, through their travels, writings, and lectures, to promote and put into practice the concept of conservation angling, regardless of the applicable phrase.

Further along this ethical pathway, a number of fly anglers have adopted the idea of *biocentric ethics* as proposed by Joseph Des Jardins in *Environmental Ethics: An Introduction to Environmental Philosophy* (1997). It supports the view that all life possesses an intrinsic value—valuable in itself and not valued simply for its use. It is argued that to view living organisms as having an inherent worth is to embrace the attitude of respect for nature. Fly anglers value the trout that they release because they may recognize in it a symbolic, cultural, or aesthetic importance that transcends its importance as a food item or trophy. I recall a story where an angler fished a local stream with a hookless fly. He was happy simply to see the trout rise to his fly. All he needed to know was that they were there!

Albert Schweitzer (1875–1965), the noted humanitarian and physician, was one of the early practitioners of biocentric ethics as epitomized by his "reverence for life" principle. While there is some debate as to whether Schweitzer wanted to assign a religious tone to his principle, Schweitzer did not envision reverence for life as some set of rules that applies to specific situations regarding life but rather a set of moral guidelines. Though he personally was against killing any other life, his principle does not directly admonish those who must make that decision. Schweitzer would have argued that the angler deciding to keep a fish should be keenly aware of the responsibility of such a decision. Reverence for life makes us reluctant to take a life randomly or with wanton callousness. While not referring to Schweitzer directly, Nick Lyons echoes a similar sentiment: "The fly-fishers' sport demands more of him. He is generally less interested in how many fish he catches than in how they were caught" (1989, 185).

But it is the *how* that we must focus on now, because, after the fish itself, the emphasis on fly-fishing must be on the fly. A number of writers, including Ted Leeson (1994), have argued that the fly is central and primary to the art and science of fly-fishing. So central is the fly to the sport that much of the jargon and terminology associated with fly-fishing originated with evolution of fly patterns (Browning 1998).

The dictionary defines a fly as "1. Any of numerous winged insects of the order Diptera, 2. Any of the various other flying insects such as the caddis fly." The early flies were probably imitations of flying winged insects, since these were most readily observable and obtainable to the angler. Most present-day fly patterns attempt to imitate the many distinctive stages of insect and other life seen on and within the water. For example, trout flies are tied to resemble the various insects that these fish eat, as well as minnows and other invertebrates. Other flies that deviate from attempting to copy nature are referred to simply as attractors. These flies look like nothing seen in nature, and it is theorized that they provoke the striking reflex in fish. Whether one is a purist and wants to try fishing detailed imitations of the aquatic world or simply to fish a fly that is aesthetically pleasing, there are four main types of flies for salmonids (trout and salmon): dry, wet, nymph, and streamer. An initial classification divides the dry flies into those that float and the wet, nymph, and streamer flies into those that sink. In a later section, we deal in depth with the discipline of aquatic entomology, but at present a cursory overview will suffice to develop our historical perspective of the fly.

FIG. 1. Flies

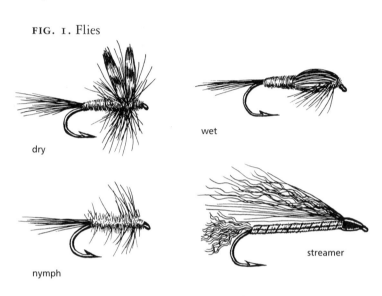

dry

wet

nymph

streamer

DRY FLY. The initial motivation for dry-fly (fig. 1) fishing was based upon the observation that certain aquatic insects, during a particular stage in their life cycle, are found floating in the surface water film. George Pulman first described this method in 1841 with the publication of *Vade Mecum of Fly Fishing for Trout.* By the late 1880s the dry fly was well known but not universally adopted by fly anglers. Essentially, the dry fly of this period did not lend itself to efficient fishing. When cast, these flies settled either on their side or upside down on the water surface. In addition, instead of floating on the water surface, they became waterlogged and sank in short order. With advances in fly-tying material, the popularity of dry-fly-fishing spread rapidly throughout southern England on the chalk streams of Hampshire. It literally became an obsession with English anglers with the publication of Frederic Halford's book, *Floating Flies and How to Dress*

Them (1886). The earliest British writers placed an emphasis on aesthetics, and its highest form was in the use of the dry fly. There are angling clubs in England that even today *only* allow trout be fished using the dry fly. The impact of dry-fly-fishing in England was soon felt in the United States, mainly through the efforts of Theodore Gordon. With the introduction of his "quill gordon" fly, it gave American flytiers the confidence to step out from the shadow of the English school of fly-tying (Schullery 1999). In the nearly 150-year history of the dry fly, innumerable refinements and variations (bivisibles, parachutes, spent wings) have taken place, mainly in the identification of additional insect species to be imitated by these flies.

The key to successful dry-fly-fishing is the ability of the fly to imitate minute floating aquatic organisms. One of the key variables that determines the ability of an object to float is the ratio of its surface area (proportional to the square of its radius) of the object to its volume (proportional to the cube of its radius). Objects that have large surface areas in relation to their volume are effective floaters. (To increase the ability to float in a pool, one simple technique is to spread the arms out from the body, effectively increasing the surface area.) Since they have a relatively high area-to-volume ratio, small fly patterns have slow settling rates and relatively high drag-per-unit volume. The wings and hackles of a dry fly are attached so that they radiate outward from the body. For the reader who wants to pursue the topic of the dry-fly construction in greater depth, there are numerous guides on this topic found in local bookstores or fly shops.

WET FLY AND NYMPH. As compared to dry flies, wet flies (fig. 1) are generally more sparsely constructed to aid in their sinking below the water surface. Fishing with wet flies is the oldest form of fly-fishing, its existence predating the advent and use of dry flies. Its early arrival on the fly-fishing scene is due in part to its effectiveness in catching fish. But there is still debate as to why at times it can be so productive, since it raises the question of what this fly imitates in nature. For example, it is hypothesized that wet flies are sometimes mistaken for drowning insects by fish. Many patterns have been documented as early as 1836 in Alfred Ronalds's book *Fly Fisher's Entomology*. Vincent Marino's book, *In the Ring of the Rise* (1976), characterized Ronald as a new breed of angler-entomologist for his time, since he was also deeply interested in the role of aquatic optics on a fish's visual acuity. Considering the success of these classical patterns in catching fish, they are still widely used by the modern-day angler.

As we will develop further in the section on aquatic insects, nymphs (fig. 1) represent a distinctive stage in the life cycle of numerous aquatic insects. Fishing with nymphs started about the same time as dry-fly-fishing. In attempting to catch particularly wary brown trout in the English town of Itchen, G. Skues observed that these trout were receptive to a particular nymph that drifted just below the water surface. In 1895, while experimenting with numerous fly patterns, he developed the first prototype nymph pattern. In his book *Nymph Fishing for Chalkstream Trout* (1939) he elucidates his technique for successful nymph fishing. Ultimately, Skues's technique reached the United States, where it was readily embraced by the likes of James Leisenring, the "father" of American nymph fishing. Another Englishmen, Frank Sawyer, introduced in the 1950s a nymph technique for catching deepwater fish. By slightly increasing the weight of the nymph, the fly was able to sink deeper into the water column to where the fish would be holding. He also reduced the number of nymph patterns to a few elementary imitative forms that were ideally suited for this type of fishing. As echoed by Tom Rosenbauer, a fly-fishing consultant for the Orvis Company, one doesn't need thousands of nymph patterns to catch fish. Keep it simple by using a general copy of the size, shape, and color of whatever the fish are feeding on. Nymphs have the potential to be the most valuable addition to your arsenal of flies because many nymphs are available in trout streams on a year-round basis.

STREAMERS. These flies are generally representations of larger prey that may be the forage for big predators. The term *streamer* may be rather limiting, since it generally is associated with long, skinny flies (fig. 1) tied to imitate a small baitfish, such as a minnow. However, there are many other patterns that are close imitators of other natural organisms—muddlers, sculpins, and leeches. Then there are those streamers, developed by the fertile imagination of a flytier, that have no analog in nature but have proven effective due to their color or movement or the confidence of the angler.

Ancient streamers have been found in various localities, having originated throughout the world. For example, around 250 years ago, fishermen in the mountainous regions of Lapland constructed extremely simple streamers tied to the hooks of reindeer horn (Frohlich and Johansson 1988). Other streamers (featherclad bone hooks), developed in New Zealand, were in use by the native population long before the Europeans brought trout and salmon to these islands. Though they were used in Maine in the beginning of the twentieth century to imitate the smelt that salmon feed on, the English predate this usage by about fifty years when they used feathered streamers in pursuing saltwater species. Modern streamer fishing owes its origin to the efforts of many North American fly anglers. In particular, the versatile Theodore Gordon around 1880 developed a streamer that was the prototype for the current bucktail pattern, which he employed successfully on the Neversink River. As with many aspects of fly-fishing, the boundaries of fly development and tying are flexible—limited only by one's imagination and creativity. Probably in no area of fly-fishing is human ingenuity and productivity more in evidence than, as we will see in the next chapter, in the fly rod.

Fly Rods: Types and Mechanical Properties

A FRIEND HAS PIQUED YOUR INTEREST IN FLY-fishing, and you're ready to purchase your first fly rod. Looking through the multitude of tackle catalogs, you are dismayed at the number and types of fly rods on the market and the associated jargon used to describe these rods. For example, what does it mean when the catalog description for a fly rod includes the following: "A perfectly loading, 9-foot, medium-action, 7-weight"? The answer to this question is important because you want a rod that performs well and one that you can feel comfortable with for a long time. The rod needs to perform a number of tasks in fly-fishing: casting, repositioning your line on the water, and playing a hooked fish. Your anxiety is heightened even more when you see that the price of a fly rod can be hundreds of dollars! If you've ever experienced the above scenario, or know someone who has, let's try to eliminate some of this confusion.

Rods are designed by manufacturers to take a certain weight line. For example, a "5-weight rod" takes a 5-weight line; a "9-weight rod" takes a 9-weight line. At first, it may seem odd to designate a rod by its fly line. But one of the primary tasks of the rod is to cast the line, and there is a positive correlation between overall rod size and line weight. What exactly does the word *weight* mean with regard to line dimensions? The number designation of each weight is the mass in grains (437.5 grains = 1 ounce) of the first 30 feet of line. (Though the terms *weight* and *mass* are often considered to be synonymous, weight in this context has a totally different meaning from a physics perspective—see technical focus.)

A 3-weight line may have a mass of 100 grains compared to a mass of 380 grains for a 12-weight line. This classification system was initiated by the American Fishing Tackle Manufacturers Association in 1961 and has been universally adopted throughout the world. Before 1961, line diameters were used to classify fly lines, with letters of the alphabet corresponding to particular diameters. This worked well when all fly lines were made of silk, so there was a positive relationship between diameter and mass. But with the advent of lines of varying diameter to meet new angling situations, this system was ultimately scrapped in favor of the present method of classification.

Modern-day rods range in size from 1-weight to 15-weight. But which rod do you select? The answer to that question depends upon the type of fishing that you will be doing and hence the fish you are pursuing. Keep in mind that in flyfishing, the mass of the line delivers the fly when you cast. Larger flies are generally heavier and more wind-resistant than smaller flies. In order to cast these flies, a heavier line and rod are needed. In pursuing large fish you need a rod that is capable of delivering both the larger flies and line to the quarry. On a small mountain stream, in pursuit of trout, a 4- to 5-weight rod is appropriate. Attempting to entice a 100-pound tarpon on the tropical flats would require a 12- or 13-weight rod. Table 1 shows some typical species matched to the appropriate rod/line weight. Though higher-weight rods could cast lower-weight lines, the reverse is not true. The smaller, lighter rod is overmatched for the bulkier fly line. Determine your target fish, and be consistent in matching the fly rod, line, and fly together.

As noted in the previous chapter, the use of rods in angling has been around for centuries. But, as with most technological advances, fly-rod development had rather humble beginnings. Early fly anglers used rods that were in some cases no more than cut saplings. The application of technology to the sport of fly-fishing led to advances in the materials used in fly rods. Rod materials were originally selected for their strength and the ease with which they could be converted into functioning rods. Solid wood rods were constructed from such

TABLE 1. Fly rod weights matched to type of fish

Weights	Type of Fish
1, 2, 3, 4	Panfish, small trout (1 to 3 lb)
5, 6, 7	Trout, small-mouth bass (4 to 8 lb)
8, 9	Large-mouth bass, salmon (10 to 30 lb)
10, 11, 12, 13	Salmon, tarpon (50 to 150 lb)
14, 15	Large tuna, marlin (200 to 400 lb)

hardwoods as ash, ironwood, lancewood, and greenheart. Generally, these early rods were approximately 12 to 15 feet in length and had four sections, with the lower portion made of ash and the top made of springy, supple lancewood. While they had the advantage of being relatively easy to turn on a lathe and were strong and flexible, their heaviness was a major drawback.

The use of bamboo proved to be the next major step in rod development. These bamboo rods, though hollow, concentrated their strongest fibers near the outside surface of the rod. While the problem of heaviness was alleviated, this wild-growing cane exhibited diameters or tapers that were often not suitable for fly-rod performance. Cutting individual strips of bamboo, tapering each of the strips on a milling machine to tolerances of a few thousandths of an inch, and gluing them together achieved more uniform properties of rods. Through trial and error, the six-strip bamboo rod emerged as the standard in its class. Hiram Lewis Leonard is given credit as the designer and builder of the hexagonal split-cane fly rod. Bamboo rods are available today, and some fly anglers are adamant as to their superiority to other rods. Bliss Perry in his writings extols the virtue of fine equipment: "A 3 or 4 ounce split-bamboo rod, with a well-balanced reel, a tapered casting line, a leader of proper fineness and a well-tied fly or flies, is one of the most perfectly designed and executed triumphs of human artisanship. A violin is but little better" (1927, 35). Since most of the steps involved in making a bamboo rod are labor intensive, they commonly come with price tags of more than a thousand dollars! Throughout the first part of the twentieth century, bamboo was the prime material in the construction of fly rods—from delicate trout rods to robust saltwater rods. Though manufacturers experimented with other types of wood and even tubular steel, these materials did not lend themselves to producing quality fly rods.

The first synthetic material to be utilized in rods, starting in the 1940s, was fiberglass, a composite material consisting of glass fibers in a resin. The use of more than one material to construct a rod has the significant advantage of increasing its toughness; that is, its ability to tolerate cracks without breaking. The science intrinsic to the construction of fiberglass rods is essentially based on one of the oldest composite materials, dating back thousands of years—adobe bricks, a mixture of straw and mud. Their toughness is due to the inclusion of the straw. When a crack appears in a brick, it does not grow very long before it intersects a straw. Simply, the straw blunts the end of the crack by reducing the stress concentrations at the crack tip. Since the straws are arranged randomly, no crack can progress very far before meeting another straw, so no crack can grow large enough to cause structural failure of the brick (McGowan 1999). Since fly rods invariably get scratched in spite of our efforts to protect them, and these scratches can grow into cracks, the damage is minimized because of the composite nature of the rod.

These initial fiberglass rods were solid in their construction, and the problem of heaviness again limited their acceptance. By the 1950s, fiberglass fly rods were hollow and more consistent in their material properties throughout the length of the rod. They were formed by wrapping a sheet of fiberglass, under pressure, around a stainless-steel form or mandrel shaped to determine the cross-sectional shape or taper of the rod. Once the mandrel is removed, the finished product is a hollow fly rod. Since these rods could be manufactured at a much lower cost than bamboo rods and their properties of length, diameter, and taper could be easily controlled and reproduced, hollow fiberglass rods soon found their way onto the marketplace.

The next step in the evolution of fly-rod construction was the use of graphite—a soft steel-gray-to-black form of carbon. As used in fly-rod construction, graphite is manufactured in big rolls or sheets. Upon closer inspection of one of these sheets, you can see the components of the rod blank—thousands of tiny, linear filaments of graphite held together by an epoxy resin. This combination is often referred to as a *prepeg*— probably for graphite pre-pregnated with resin. The resin is literally the glue that holds everything together in a finished rod. If the manufacturer did not give appropriate care to the chemical makeup of the resin, then the resultant product would be a rod that would unduly twist and ultimately break, especially if subjected to high temperatures. This is as good a reason as any for not storing a fly rod in the back window of the car on a hot summer day. There is another thin layer of either fiberglass or graphite fibers, called the *scrim,* running crosswise to the prepeg that prevents the linear graphite fibers from separating, thus reinforcing the strength of the rod.

The graphite material is wrapped around a mandrel, along with resins, then covered with a heat-shrink tape, and baked in an oven. The heat of the oven causes the resins to liquefy and penetrate throughout the graphite and scrim. After cooling, the tape and the mandrel are removed, leaving a basic rod blank. Some companies may spray the rod with a type of finish coat. The resulting product is an extremely light fly rod with a tensile strength greater than steel. While weight differences in a small trout rod will not be significant regardless of the rod material, as you move up in rod size the difference can be important. A 9-foot bamboo salmon rod may weigh 7 ounces, a fiberglass rod almost 6 ounces, and a graphite rod only 3 ounces. Though on the surface these differences seem negligible, after numerous casts throughout the day, a tired arm and wrist will result from casting a relatively heavy rod compared to a featherweight graphite rod.

The use of a rod of any type must provide some advantage to the angler; otherwise why expend the effort and expense of owning a rod? A fly rod reduced to its essential elements is basically a lever. A lever is a rigid bar that is free to pivot about a fixed point, the fulcrum. Whether it is a wrench to tighten a bolt or a bar to remove a nail, a lever provides the user with a mechanical advantage in achieving the task. In the case of the crowbar, the effort force (the amount of effort being applied to the task at hand) to remove the nail is multiplied over the distance the effort is applied. As long as the effort force is applied to a greater distance from the fulcrum than the resistance force, a mechanical advantage is obtained—the nail is pulled out more easily than if we used our hands alone. For a fly rod, the fulcrum is at the end (butt) of the rod where you are holding it. At the top (tip) of the rod is the resistance, hopefully a big fish (fig. 2). The other hand applies the effort force as you pull back on the rod. In this case you need move your effort force only a short distance to make the tip of the rod move a greater distance. As shown in figure 3, the rod is initially in position one. Now, if the fly angler exerts an effort and lifts the rod to position two, note the greater angular distance the rod has swept through at the tip compared to the butt of the rod. Essentially, a lever (fly rod) of this type multiplies the distance through which the effort force moves.

FIG. 2. The fly rod viewed as a lever

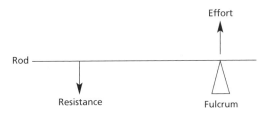

FIG. 3. Comparison of the angular distance traveled by the butt versus the tip of the rod

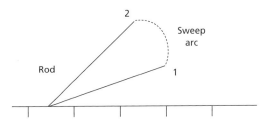

In playing a fish, the advantage achieved is that more line is retrieved at the rod tip for limited movement of the hands positioned near the rod butt.

In addition to considering the appropriate rod weight for the fishing situation, the astute angler should seriously study the advantages achieved by using a long rod over a short rod. Longer rods will "sweep out" a greater distance at the tip of the rod than shorter rods for the same corresponding distance moved at the rod butt. Consider two rods equal in all other aspects except length. One is 10 feet long, and the other is 5 feet long. Both rods are lifted from the horizontal to an angle of 45 degrees (fig. 4). Note the difference in vertical distance that the longer rod sweeps out. (The distance traveled by the rod tip is not actually a straight line but has an arc path.) Simple trigonometric calculations show the distances to be approximately 7 feet and 3.5 feet for the long and short rod, respectively.

FIG. 4. Comparison of the vertical distance traveled by a long versus a short rod

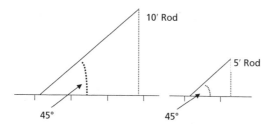

One of the challenges of fly-fishing is adjusting to changing conditions that occur during the course of an angling outing. The ability of the angler to recognize and overcome these obstacles can be the difference between a successful fishing outing versus one that leaves the angler wondering why he didn't take up golf. Though we will delve into it in more detail in later chapters, the flow of water across a stream is not uniform with regard to its speed. Simply, there are fast and slow currents that will drag the angler's line at an uneven pace once it has been cast upon the water to the waiting trout. This will lead to an unnatural movement of the fly and generally

THE SCIENCE OF FLY-FISHING

the angler's offering being spurned by the trout. The angler needs to recognize that the line and fly must literally "go with the flow." The angler lifting line from the water and repositioning the line in relation to the varying current speed can accomplish this. Because of its increased leverage, a long rod can easily lift more line from the water surface than a short rod. Most trout fly rods range in length from 7½ to 8½ feet. Though shorter rods do have their place—particularly in tight casting quarters and, as we will soon discuss, in fighting a very large fish—most serious fly anglers would scoff at using rods shorter than 6 feet. On the other hand, longer rods for a particular line weight have become quite common. It is not unusual for a 4-weight line to be matched to a 9-foot rod. This is possible because of the high strength-to-mass ratio for modern graphite rods. The same 9-foot rod made of fiberglass would be quite heavy and tiresome to use in any activity that requires repetitive motion.

If a rod merely acts as a rigid lever, then a broomstick might serve as a usable fly rod. Modern fly rods bend and flex, and it is these characteristics that allow the fly angler to more efficiently and effectively fight a fish and cast the fly line. A fish that is accelerating, by changing its speed or direction, exerts a strain on the equipment. A fly rod must flex, acting like a shock absorber, to mitigate the sudden surges of the fish; otherwise we have a break-off. Unfortunately, definitions and quantification of a rod's characteristics are not uniform in the literature and are often misleading. Most fly anglers use the term *action* to describe the way a fly rod flexes under stress. Fast-action rods flex in only the top 25 percent of the rod. Slow-action rods flex throughout the length of rod. But from a scientific perspective; the word *action* has no quantitative basis in the physical science.

Through a series of articles in the *American Fly Fisher* during the late 1980s, Graig Spolek employed the terms *stiffness* and *frequency* to describe the mechanical properties of a fly rod. His argument is based on the fact that these terms have precise definitions and can be measured quantitatively. Stiffness is a measure of how much a rod deflects when a load (mass) is applied to it. The load may be from the line during the casting motion or from the retrieval of the fish.

The stiffness of rod depends upon the dimensions of the rod and its material. The stiffness of rod is inversely proportional to its length. Specifically, the stiffness varies inversely to the length squared. All other factors being the same, a 5-foot rod would be four times as rigid as a 10-foot rod. In attempting to fight a very heavy fish, shorter rods have a distinct mechanical advantage over longer rods. The primary objective in fighting a large fish is simply to overcome its resistance, lift, and gain some line. If the rod has an excessive bend to it under load, the advantage provided to the angler from using the rod as a lever is minimized. With a fish like a large salmon, the angler might not be able to exert enough force at the butt section to simply lift the fish. In this case the advantage switches to the fish.

The following argument presents another perspective on short versus long rods in fighting a large fish. Note in figure 5 that, in order to lift both rods the same distance at the tip, I would have to lift the 5-foot rod though a greater vertical distance at the butt of the rod than for the 10-foot rod. However, the force applied to the butt section of the 5-foot rod would be *less* than that for the 10-foot rod. Let's see why the above statements are true. Work is essentially a form of energy—like solar and wind energy. (A more mathematical approach to the concept of work is given in the Technical Focus section below.) In the case of the fly rod as a lever, as in many scenarios in physics, there must be a conservation of energy. (Note that the meaning of *conservation* as used here is not synonymous with the common usage of modest consumption of a resource.) In our case, the energy (work) at the tip must be equivalent (conserved) to the energy exerted at the butt. Since the 5-foot fly rod moves through a greater distance at the butt section than the 10-foot rod, the amount of force needed to lift the salmon is less for the 5-foot rod, but the work (energy) will be the same.

The diameter of a rod also influences how much a rod will deflect under a load. Large-diameter rods are stiffer than small-diameter rods, with the stiffness being proportional to the

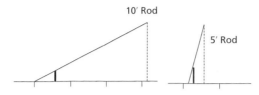

FIG. 5. Comparison of the distance traveled at the butt section for a long versus short rod

quadruple of the diameter. Therefore, even relatively tiny changes in the rod's diameter can have a profound influence on the stiffness of the rod. If you look carefully at a fly rod, you will notice that the diameter is not constant over its entire length. Fly rods have a decreasing diameter with length that is referred to as its taper. It is obvious then that the nature of the taper will also affect the stiffness. Rods that have a uniform taper are those where the diameter decreases at a constant rate over the length of the rod. For rods of this type, the taper can be quantified as the ratio of tip diameter to butt diameter. The lower the ratio, the more limber the rod.

Whether the material is fiberglass, bamboo, or graphite, each has its own inherent rigidity that is referred to as the *modulus of elasticity,* or simply *modulus.* The modulus of graphite is considerably higher than that of fiberglass—quite simply, it is more rigid. Though we will discuss the effect of rod material, hence flexibility, on the casting stroke in the next chapter, one advantage of graphite rods is that their diameter can be decreased to obtain the same stiffness as a comparable fiberglass rod. This dimensional change means less overall heft to the graphite rod. On the negative side, increased modulus results in increased cost to the consumer, since the process involved in creating very high-modulus graphite rods is a costly one. Also, increased modulus results in rods that are somewhat brittle and more likely to break from impacts like dropping the rod on a hard surface. While standard graphite is rated at 33 million modulus, top-of-the-line graphite rods have a rating of 65 million modulus.

Purchasing a fly rod from a discount store to save a few bucks may be a poor decision because of how the total rod, including its guides, was put together. When a rod is bent or placed in an arc, as in fighting a fish, the rod will bend naturally along a certain axis called the spline (literally the spine or backbone of the rod). All tubular rods have a spline to some degree. The "perfect" blank would not have one, but current manufacturing processes do not allow for this. A poorly constructed rod will have its guides sitting off in all different directions from the way the rod was actually bending. This defect can affect the casting performance of the rod as well as influence the structural integrity of the rod when the rod is severely bent due to the pressure applied by a big fish. If these rods had been built properly, the guides would be positioned in line with the spline.

We have previously discussed that one of the drawbacks of the early fly rods was their excessive weight because they were solid in construction. However, there appears to be a movement initiated by some rod manufacturers to return to the solid rod. One of the disadvantages of the tubular rod as pointed out by Briscoe (2001) is that it is designed to bend or load "perfectly" at only a specified line length. For example, our 9-foot medium-action rod, from above, is designed to "load perfectly" at about 36 inches below its tip with let's say 30 feet of line in the air from the casting stroke. But if the caster has 45 feet or 20 feet of line in the air, or anything besides the designated 30 feet, it will load less perfectly. The rod will try to bend around its designed parameter, but it won't be "perfect." This is why a caster may feel "out of rhythm" with the rod during the casting stroke. It is claimed that solid rods eliminate this problem because the mechanical properties inherent to a solid rod allow it to flex or bend perfectly in accordance with the load.

However, on the downside, tubular rods are stronger than solid rods of the same mass. As a solid rod bends, it experiences various stresses—tension on the top section of the rod and compression on the underside (fig. 6). If we were to take an imaginary probe and measure stresses in the rod, we would find that the tensional stress was at a maximum at the top edge and decreased incrementally moving toward the center

THE SCIENCE OF FLY-FISHING

FIG. 6. A rod in tension and compression

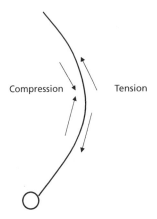

Compression   Tension

of the rod, ultimately reaching a zero value in the middle. Continued measurements with our probe would show compressive stresses increasing from the middle outward to the bottom of the rod, reaching a maximum at the bottom edge. The point of zero stress is referred to as the neutral axis. The implication of the neutral axis is that the stresses are zero at the center of the rod when it is bending, so there is *no need for any material to be there.* Conversely, the stresses are maximal at the outer edges of the rod, so this is where most of the material should be concentrated, as it is in a tubular rod. Having a tubular rod with the largest possible diameter places the material at a maximum distance from the neutral axis where it most needed to resist the bending loads—hence its strength and stiffness are maximized. However, as the diameter increases, the walls of the tube become progressively thinner, meaning there is less material to take the load. Ultimately, a point is reached when the advantage of having a large diameter to mitigate stresses on the rod's surfaces is offset by the tendency of the tube to fail due to buckling—folds appear in the material being loaded, ultimately causing it to break (McGowan 1999). Accordingly, rod manufacturers realize that there is an optimal wall thickness that gives the tube its maximum strength under a given loading regime. What this means is that a 4-weight line that has been designed for a load equivalent to a trout's mass (2 to 3 pounds) will probably fail structurally if used to tackle large salmon (50 to 60 pounds). Keep in mind that these high-performance and costly rods have been designed with a relatively small margin between the stresses of normal usage and the stress at which the rod will break.

In order to understand the next characteristic of a rod that affects its performance, a brief review of some common physics terms pertaining to motion is in order. Any type of motion that repeats itself over the same time is *periodic*. If the motion is back and forth over the same path, it is called *oscillatory*. An oscillation is one round trip of the motion. The time required for one oscillation is called the *period* (T). The *frequency* (f) of the motion is the number of oscillations per unit of time.

The concept of oscillations or vibrations can be demonstrated by a multitude of phenomena both in the natural and physical world. A taut spring that is released will vibrate until its motion is damped out by restraining forces. The vibrations of the spring will occur over many frequencies but, because of its mechanical properties, will have a primary frequency of oscillation—the fundamental frequency. The fundamental frequency has been shown to be the most important one in the casting stroke. As we will soon see, an efficient casting stroke generates maximum line speed. The line speed during casting depends upon the fundamental frequency of the rod, all other factors being equal. Rods that have a high fundamental frequency will deliver a faster line speed than similar rods with a low frequency.

A rod's frequency is dependent upon its stiffness and the distribution of its mass. With regard to the former, an increase in stiffness accounts for a higher fundamental frequency. In other words, the dimensions and material of the rod have a profound influence on the rod's frequency, assuming they have no effect on the rod's mass distribution. Obviously, these parameters do change the mass and its distribution along the rod. The crux of the argument is that the frequency cannot be predicted solely from the stiffness. Two rods with exactly the same stiffness may have different frequencies.

In summary, the performance of a rod can depend upon a myriad of factors, but if an angler does her homework before purchasing a rod, then she can select a rod that is matched to her angling skills and checkbook. Now let's get up to speed with the most basic fly-angling skill—fly casting.

Technical Focus

Previously, I introduced the concept of force without defining the term in any rigorous manner. Though we probably have an intuitive understanding of this concept, let's proceed to the laws governing the motion of an object. Simply, any force is a push or pull. If we push an object, the object will be accelerated. Acceleration is the speeding up, the slowing down, or the change in direction of an object. This can be expressed as the fundamental equation of classical mechanics

$$a = F/m$$

where a is acceleration, F is force, and m is mass. In qualitative terms, this equation states that the acceleration of an object is directly proportional to the net force acting on the body and inversely proportional to the mass of the object, as in the direction of the net force. Rewriting the above expression, we obtain the more familiar equation

$$F = ma.$$

A force exerted on an object equals its mass times the acceleration produced.

If a 2-pound trout is to accelerate from rest to a speed of 3 feet per second (not very fast) in a second (3 ft/sec²), the force exerted on the fish is 6 lb ft/sec² or, through arithmetic conversion, 0.2 pounds of force. (The reader should be aware that the term *pound* is a British unit of force and not to be confused with the same usage when applied to the mass of an object.) For reference, 0.2 pounds is approximately equal to the force exerted by a baseball in one's hand. Obviously, the greater the mass and/or acceleration, the greater the force exerted on the fish. A 90-pound chinook salmon (the all-tackle world record is over 97 pounds) achieving an acceleration of 20 ft/sec² has a corresponding force of 53 pounds. Our initial task as an angler is to decrease the acceleration of the fleeing fish. The angler exerting an equal but opposing force on the fish accomplishes this; that is, a pulling force is exerted on the fish. If the angler simply pulls back 180 degrees to the run of the fish, the rod is not providing any mechanical advantage to the angler. It's simply a tug-of-war between the fish and the angler. Though the above scenario is not totally realistic, since the acceleration of the fish is not constant but decreases rapidly and the angler would use the drag of the reel to slow the forward motion of the fish, it does illustrate the relative forces that are involved in fighting a fish. In the above scenario, where the force pushing the fish forward is just balanced by the pulling force of the angler, we have not stopped the fish dead in the water—it's still pulling line off the reel! Its acceleration is zero, but it is now moving at a constant speed away from the angler. To stop the forward motion of the fish, the angler has to apply an even greater force than before.

Now let's tie together the concept of force and the rod as a lever. As a fly rod is lifted from the horizontal plane to the vertical plane, the object being lifted experiences a rotational acceleration as a result of the "sweeping" motion of the rod tip. The rotational analog of force is torque that can be expressed mathematically as

$$T = rF$$

where r is the vector displacement from the origin to the point of application of the force. The magnitude of the vector quantity can be expressed as

$$T = rF(\sin A)$$

where A is the angle between r and F. In figure 7 note a force F is applied at P, a point displaced r from the origin. The force makes an angle A with radius vector r. The torque about the origin (O) is shown. The direction of the torque is perpendicular to the plane formed by r and F.

Notice that the torque produced depends upon the magnitude of the effort force (F), point of application (r) of the

FIG. 7. Representation of the torque (*T*) about an origin (*O*) when a force (*F*) is applied at a distance (*r*) from the origin and at an angle (*A*) to the distance vector

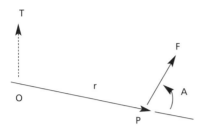

force relative to the origin, and the direction of the force (*A*). With regard to the first two variables, the greater the effort force applied over a greater distance, the greater the torque. If the force acts through the origin (*r* = *o*), no matter what its magnitude, the torque about the origin is zero. Also, *F* times the sin *A* is the magnitude of the component of *F* perpendicular to *r*. From the above equation, only this component of *F* contributes to the torque. In particular, when the angle *A* equals zero, there is no perpendicular component; hence the line of action of the force passes through the origin, and the torque is zero

$$T = rF(\sin o) = o.$$

(From trigonometry the sin o is zero.) This result would be similar to trying to loosen a nut by pulling on the wrench along its long axis. If there is a perpendicular component to the force, angle *A* is 90 degrees; the torque about the origin is a maximum, since the sine of 90 degrees is one. We now attempt to turn the wrench to loosen the nut.

What does all of the above discussion mean to the fly angler? Recall that the angler is essentially attempting to overcome the resistance force of the fish by counteracting with an effort force. If the angler pulls vertically on the rod in the opposite direction of the resistance being applied by the fish, the force applied by the angler is 90 degrees to the long axis of the rod; that is, the force multiplied by the sine of the angle is at a maximum. Obviously, pulling at any other angle minimizes this component of the torque. At the same time the angler is pulling back, the butt of the rod is placed against his mid-section—this becomes the origin. The higher the angler positions his hands on the rod from the origin, then the angler is producing the optimum condition to maximize the torque—hence the pressure brought to bear on the fish.

If the angler is ultimately to retrieve the fish either to the riverbank or boat, enough force must be exerted to move the fish the required distance. We now introduce the concept of work. From a physics perspective, the amount of work done in moving an object is equal to the magnitude of the force applied to the object multiplied by the distance through which the force is exerted. The relationship can be expressed as

$$W = Fd.$$

If we do not move the object (fish), then the work done is zero, regardless of the magnitude of the effort force and how much we grunt and sweat. Now, back to our intrepid angler. How much work has our angler expended in lifting a 90-pound salmon from a depth of 15 feet to the surface? We will assume for simplicity of discussion that the salmon is no longer moving away from the angler and is essentially a "dead weight" in the water. We must first calculate the force exerted by a 90-pound mass before we can calculate the work. Assuming negligible water resistance, the salmon would sink to the bottom under the influence of the earth's gravity. The force of gravity on an object located at a particular point is called *weight*. To lift the 90-pound salmon against the acceleration of gravity ($g = 32$ ft/sec^2) requires the following force

$$F = mg$$

$$F = 90 \text{ lb} \times 32 \text{ ft/sec}^2 = 2,880 \text{ lb ft/sec}^2 = 86 \text{ pounds}$$

Then from the equation for work,

$$W = 86 \text{ lb} \times 15 \text{ ft} = 1,290 \text{ foot-pounds}$$

(A foot-pound of work is defined as the amount of work done when a force of one pound is exerted through a distance of one foot.) For comparison, carrying a 16-pound bowling ball up a flight of stairs (13 feet) requires only 210 foot-pounds of work. Fighting a big fish is both literally and figuratively "hard work." The constant force acting on an object may not be in the direction in which the object moves. For example, if we use a rope to pull a sled over a flat field, we are actually pulling at an angle to the horizontal surface (fig. 8). If we want to move our sled in the horizontal direction but the force di-

FIG. 8. Movement of an object in direction (*d*)
in response to application of force (*F*)

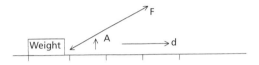

rected on the sled is 30 degrees from the horizontal plane, then we would have to exert a greater force than if the exerted force was in the same direction we want the sled to move. If the force increases, so does the work. Our previous relationship is modified as follows,

$$W = Fd/\cos A$$

where *cos* is the trigonometric cosine function and *A* is the angle between the exerted force and the desired direction of movement. Now if our angler is pulling on the salmon at an angle of 45 degrees from the vertical, instead of straight up, the work increases to 1,842 foot-pounds—a 42 percent increase. Charter boat captains will often aid an angler fighting a very large fish by "backing down the boat"; that is, repositioning it so that the angler is not pulling at a severe angle to the fish.

THREE

The Physics of Fly Casting

THE CASTING OF THE FLY LINE IS A FUNDAMENTAL skill that should be mastered in order to be a competent fly-fisher. As opposed to spinning tackle, where the weight of the lure propels the line forward, it is the mass of the fly line that delivers the fly to the fish. Many flies are designed to imitate floating insects. They are very light and have a relatively large surface area to aid in floating within the surface film of the water. Because of this "bulkiness" the forward motion of the fly is greatly impeded by air resistance. For example, Spolek (1986) states that to propel a fly 65 feet without the aid of line would require an initial speed of 313 miles per hour, an impossible condition to be met by the angler. Being able to obtain distance with the line, maintain loop control, and make a delicate presentation of the fly involve an understanding of the dynamics of an efficient fly cast. It is not my intent to instruct on how to cast. There are many excellent books that provide detailed instruction and photographs on specific movements of the angler and the rod. In addition, the reader is encouraged to take lessons from a professional in order to achieve a level of proficiency in the art of casting. Instead, in this chapter, we will attempt to address the issues of the role of the rod in casting, biomechanics of an efficient cast, and the negative effect of air resistance in obtaining casting distance.

As in the previous section on the mechanics of the fly rod, the use of terms to describe the casting of the fly line are often employed to catch the reader's attention, having no analog in the world of physics and maybe even violating physical laws of nature. It is often heard that the rod "does the work in the cast." From a physics standpoint this expression has very little relevance, since, as we have discussed, work has a specific meaning in physics. There is evidence to suggest that the above expression may have found its way into the fly-fishing literature in the erroneous comparison of the mechanical nature of a fly rod and a bow used in archery. The argument is as follows: When a rod is started forward, energy is stored in the bend of the rod, similar to the stored energy in a bow. This stored energy of the rod is then transferred to the line, in a fashion similar to energy imparted by the taut bowstring to the arrow. While a drawn bow does have elastic potential energy (energy waiting to be released and converted into kinetic energy, energy associated with moving objects), there is relatively little stored energy in the bending of the rod (Phillips 1996). The rod does not do any work! It simply acts as a flexible lever, storing some energy but essentially providing a mechanical advantage to the angler to propel the line in a more efficient manner. A good caster could cast well with a broomstick, assuming she has developed the necessary skills. A finely constructed rod makes the job easier, similar to any tool, by facilitating the casting stroke. A high-performance rod will not turn a bad caster into a top-flight caster. In addition to dispelling some myths about the role of the rod in casting, knowledge of the physical principles involved in casting can form the basis for the rational design, manufacturing, and marketing of fly rods. Let's begin our journey by analyzing the components of a complete cast.

Though there are variations of this scenario, in the initial step the angler raises the rod to lift the line off the water and propels it straight back, essentially parallel to the ground. This component of the fly line movement is called the back cast. After the line has straightened out, the caster begins the forward motion of the rod. If the line is not straight in the back, the forward motion of the rod will propel only a relatively small length of line. It is analogous to towing an object; one can get the load moving in the direction of the applied force only after the slack in the line has been removed. As the caster brings the rod forward, the line forms a loop, unrolling as it moves forward, and ultimately settling on the water.

Let's begin by discussing in detail the forward component of the casting stroke. It is the most significant part of the overall cast and embodies most of the physics associated with the motion of the line. Much of what we know about the dynamics of the fly cast has been determined by the photographic analysis of the casting motion by Ed Mosser and William Buchman (1980)—the former a tournament caster and the latter an engineer. They report that a good caster has the rod tip move in a straight line during the time the line is propelled forward. This is partially accomplished by the caster moving his hand along a line rather than merely rotating it about his wrist. Their research forms the basis for one of the underlying principles of efficient fly casting, which should be committed to memory: The line and fly go in the direction you point the rod tip during the cast. Though this statement may seem obvious, it essentially refers to Newton's second law—the acceleration of the line and fly will be in the direction of the application of the force. In addition, a high-performance rod will bend in such a way as to keep the rod tip moving in a straight line. The direction of movement is dependent on the skill of the caster who initiates and directs the cast, but the rod's bending aids in obtaining a straight trajectory. Beginning fly casters often tend to move the rod in a circular arc by bending the wrist, which creates a wide air-resistant loop. Good fly casting is not strength-related, but it is critically dependent upon timing. If the caster's motion is not in sync with the fundamental frequency of the rod, the casting stroke is not maximized and distance is sacrificed. For example, an angler using a relatively stiff rod with a high tip frequency will have to move her arm through the casting plane relatively quickly in comparison to using a limber, low-tip-frequency rod.

The photographs revealed that at the beginning of the cast there was very little bending of the rod. In contrast to some beliefs, the rod does not "load up" during this phase. About midway through the casting stroke, the acceleration of the rod tip is at a peak, resulting in maximum force applied to the line. Also at this stage, the rod bends, determined by its stiffness characteristics, to its maximum position as a result of the high line speed generated as it is pulled forward. As the caster stops the forward motion of the rod, the rod unbends and, as it springs forward, propels the line. The final stage is a reverse bend in the rod at the end of the stroke; that is, it springs back.

One of the key points in the above analysis is that the angler must accelerate the rod during the forward casting stroke to generate maximum line speed and thus distance. It is not enough to simply move your arm forward at a constant speed, since there is no force applied to the line. In the same manner that a long throw of a ball requires a long accelerating path of a full arm's length rather than a flip of the wrist, long fly casts require that the line be accelerated over long distances. In summary, the greater the acceleration and distance used to propel the line, the greater the line speed. An experienced caster such as Lefty Kreh, who has probably written and lectured more on casting techniques than anyone else, can cast a line over 100 feet. While the average angler will probably never approach this distance, nor in most fly-fishing situations is there a need for such distance, fly line speed is the dominant casting variable determining distance. For a cast of 65 feet—let's say the distance from the angler to the fish—the fly line speeds have to approach 70 miles per hour, the speed at which a major-league pitcher can throw a change-up. This speed can either increase or decrease depending upon the diameter of the line and the angler's ability to demonstrate loop control during the casting stroke. Since casting instructors constantly admonish their students to learn loop control, we will soon discuss this topic in more detail with regard to casting. To further increase line speed, advanced casters often practice the technique of *hauling*—pulling down on that portion of the line still within the rod guides. As the angler accelerates the rod, the angler simultaneously pulls down on the line. This hauling action increases the speed of the line that is in the air. The resultant speed of the line is then from the forward motion of the rod and is increased by pulling. In practice, a skilled caster employs a *double haul*—pulling down on the line during the forward and back cast—to generate increased line speed.

Long rods have a distinct mechanical advantage over short rods in achieving a long cast. Recall that a rod is essentially a lever. A 9-foot rod can be used to move the tip through 15 feet, while the caster moves his arm about 3 feet (fig. 9). With a short rod, let's say 6-foot, the distance the rod tip travels is significantly less for the same distance traveled by the arm. Longer rods will also allow the angler to hold more line in the air during the casting strokes, overall enabling the angler to again increase the distance.

FIG. 9. Distance traveled by the tip during the cast in comparison to wrist movement

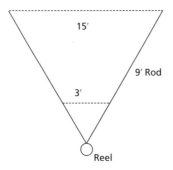

In addition to the importance of the length of the rod in determining distance, the stiffness of the rod now enters into the picture. A supple rod will subtract from the distance because the rod will bend excessively as the force builds up at the rod tip to drive the line forward. The rod tip is no longer traveling in a straight line, and, since the line and fly go in the direction you point the rod tip during the stroke, an errant cast is the result. In contrast, a stiff rod will not bend as much during application of the force, allowing for maximum fly line distance. It increases the efficiency of the casting stroke by bending just enough that the trajectory of the tip is closer to that of a straight line than that of a circular arc. A modern graphite rod, by virtue of its relatively high modulus of elasticity, is quite stiff and is not susceptible to developing a big bend, allowing a greater drive distance for the line. As we have seen, long rods allow for relatively large distances traveled by the tip during the casting stroke. But long rods may be harder to move through the casting stroke than short rods. The added weight, air resistance, and the long lever arm increasing the torque on the caster's hand all make it more difficult for the angler. The use of graphite has reduced the weight, and the thinner diameters found in graphite rods have decreased the air resistance component, but neither has changed the principal effect of the long lever arm. This problem would still exist with either long bamboo or fiberglass rods, without any of the advantages of graphite. The key to minimizing angler fatigue is to limit the number of *false casts*—the number of forward and backward strokes.

A relatively stiff graphite rod also has the advantage of having a high fundamental frequency—the rod tip has a quick recovery rate. After the angler has finished the forward casting stroke and the rod is pointing in the desired direction, the rod tip vibrates only once at the end and returns to a straight position. A rod that vibrates many times will send many secondary wavelets down the line, decreasing the efficiency of the cast.

Now let's try to tie the above discussion together from an energy perspective. (For a quantitative discussion see the Technical Focus section 1, below.) It is ultimately the energy imparted to the line that determines its speed. As the caster drives the rod forward during the casting stroke, energy is transferred almost immediately to the line. Since the rod is a flexible link between the caster and the line, the rod bends during the forward motion of the cast. As the caster runs out of distance for moving the rod tip or abruptly stops, the rod unbends, yielding some of its stored energy to the moving line. At this stage, the energy is from both the rod movement and the unbending of the rod.

In summary, the rod acts as a lever, albeit a complicated one, transferring energy supplied by the caster, storing some of the energy, and dissipating energy in the rod vibration. A relatively stiff graphite rod will not store much of its energy in its spring effect. This means that most of the energy produced by the caster will be available to transfer to the fly line. All else being equal, graphite rods cast farther than fiberglass rods.

Though we have seen the role of the rod and caster in setting the fly line in motion, let's see how the nature of the fly line comes into play with regard to casting. Though the mass of the line delivers the fly to the fish, a line's shape and construction determine how it delivers and presents the fly. One of the basic characteristics of a fly line is the design of its taper. Manufacturers design the taper by varying the thickness of the line coating—a supple synthetic material, usually polyvinyl chloride. The thickness and shape of the coating along the length of the line determines its taper. The front part of the line is generally thin to minimize the disturbance as the line settles on the water after the cast. The thickness of the line then increases over a length (generally 30 feet) of the line, called the *belly*. How the thickness varies over this portion determines the type of taper commonly found in most fly lines— weight-forward, double-taper, and shooting-taper. The remainder of the fly line is referred to as the running line. While each type of taper has its advocates and there are subtle variations of these basic designs (bass, bonefish, saltwater tapers) for specific angling situations, weight-forward tapers have the greatest applicability in casting. Having the mass of the line concentrated in the front portion of the line enables the angler to achieve a greater distance than if the fly line had a constant diameter over its entire length.

In addition to varying the line's taper to enhance its casting performance, the manufacturer can change the line's core to modify performance. For example, if the core is composed of relatively stiff material such as monofilament, the stiffness of the line will be increased, and that will allow for long casts. In contrast, if the core is made of relatively limp material such as braided dacron or nylon, casting distance is sacrificed, particularly in hot locations that exacerbate the limpness of the line. One final manufacturing step may include adding lubricants to the line coating. Combined with a hard, smooth line coating and proper taper, these lubricants reduce friction and allow for smoother, longer casts.

We are now at the stage to discuss the motion of the line itself and in particular the loop that forms in the line at the end of the casting stroke. Stopping the rod at the end of the casting stroke is the necessary factor in forming the loop. Fly anglers are forever extolling the virtues of achieving a tight loop in casting as opposed to a wide, open loop. Though tight loops will improve fly-line distance, arguments abound as to the exact reason this is so. Some argue that wide loops decrease distance because of the air resistance imposed on the larger surface area of the loop. Others postulate that the energy imparted to the fly line is spread over a wider area instead of being directed in a forward line. As in our discussions before, we will turn to a number of detailed and analytical studies (Spolek 1986, Lingard 1987) that have analyzed this problem. Fly-line motion is a rather difficult problem to come to grips with, and the authors have relied on relatively complex mathematics to express their arguments. We will take the easy way out and simplify the problem without removing its essence. The model being presented does not represent all aspects of the "real" world. Initially, the model ignores gravity and air resistance. Not too cool, but remember it's just a model that attempts to describe in part what is really happening to the fly line.

Once the angler has stopped the forward motion of the rod, the line forms a loop, with the top portion of the loop traveling forward and the bottom segment remaining stationary, since it is attached to the rod tip. As the relative length of each segment of the line changes during the cast, the loop will travel down the line until it reaches the end of the line. The line straightens, and the cast is complete (fig. 10). We again apply to our problem the very useful principle in physics— the conservation of energy. The cast begins with an initial line length, mass, and velocity. It therefore starts with a certain kinetic energy (essentially mass times the velocity squared) that, as we have seen, was imparted by the caster. As the top portion of the line unfurls, the mass of the traveling portion of the line decreases as the length decreases. Since energy must be conserved, the speed of the line must increase as it travels forward. (For the interested reader, see Technical Focus section 2, below, which adds a "dash" of mathematics to season our discussion.)

FIG. 10. Decreasing length of top portion of fly line as line rolls out during cast

The discussion above considers a fly line that has a uniform diameter over its entire length. How does the velocity change with a tapered line? Even though the total mass of the line does not change compared to that of a level line, a forward-tapered line has a significant portion of the mass in the belly of the line. As we have just seen, the kinetic energy, originally in the entire traveling portion of the fly line, gets concentrated into an ever-shrinking portion of the line remaining. This results in the tip of the line increasing its speed rapidly. In a tapered line, the energy gets concentrated even faster at the tip because the cross-sectional area of the tip is much smaller than the belly portion. The result is a speedup of the line at the tip compared to a level line. Let's use the example of a whip in comparison to our tapered line. Because the whip is much heavier and much more tapered than the fly line, and the butt end, which corresponds to the rod tip, is moving backward, the wielder of the whip can generate very high tip speeds, approaching the speed of sound—the whip "cracks." Though high fly-line speeds are desirable, the "cracking" of the line is not desirable, since it can lead to the fly snapping off the end of the line!

The effects of air resistance are not negligible and now need to be included in our discussion. The main result is that the kinetic energy of the fly line will decrease continuously as the

THE SCIENCE OF FLY-FISHING

line unrolls due to the dissipative effect of friction. Though we probably can already guess the outcome, the effect of air resistance is to decrease the line speed as compared to the scenario of no resistance. The main parts of the cast that contribute to this resistance are the loop, the traveling line, and the fly. Research has shown that, of these three, the resistance on the loop dominates the overall loss of energy. The resistance on the traveling line can be greater than on the loop when the traveling line is long, but it decreases continuously as this portion shortens. The resistance on the loop remains constant, and its integrative effects over the duration of the cast can be a significant factor in decreasing line speed. The main loop variable that comes into play is the loop diameter—vertical distance from the traveling to the stationary portion of the line. As demonstrated by Spolek (1986), the initial line velocity needed to deliver a fly at a speed of 70 miles per hour upon completion of the cast increases dramatically as loop diameter increases, regardless of the line taper. For example, with a loop diameter of 3.5 feet, the initial velocity is 58 miles per hour but with a loop diameter of 7 feet increases to 184 miles per hour! A tight loop, with a small diameter, is what every fly caster should aim for in attempting to minimize air resistance. While it is physically impossible to cast a zero-diameter loop, there is significant advantage to a small-as-possible loop: long, efficient casts. Beginner casters are often frustrated that, even though their mechanics appear to be sound, the fly line at the end of the casting stroke does not shoot straight out but gathers up in an embarrassing clump at their feet. From a physics perspective, it's fairly simple to analyze what happened: the opposing force of air resistance was greater than the force imparted to the rod by the angler. Maintaining a tight loop and smartly accelerating the rod over the distance stroke will result in casting like a professional.

In addition to proper casting mechanics, line hauling, and loop control, one other technique to increase distance is *shooting line*. It essentially entails pulling off 10 or more feet of line from your reel, keeping it in reserve as coils hanging at your feet, lightly holding this line in your noncasting hand, and releasing this additional line on the forward cast. The key point is to stop your rod smartly after the acceleration stroke so that the mass of the line outside the rod guides pulls this reserved line through the guides. With the use of relatively frictionless snake guides, replacing the minuscule flip-ring guides in the 1890s, came the opportunity to *shoot a line*. The origin of this term probably can be found in a nautical context, much like throwing a line in a man-overboard situation. As navies modernized, a rifle-like device was used to deliver (shoot?) line (rope) to another ship so that a larger line could be hauled over. This was done to transfer or rescue sailors between ships. Whatever its origin, this technique ties up our discussion on the essential physics of basic fly casting. At this stage, we have been exposed to the fundamental principles intrinsic to any number of other casts that skilled anglers include in their repertoire. Let's take the next step.

Casts such as the steeple cast, parachute cast, puddle cast, curve cast, and roll cast have been developed and refined to help the angler overcome difficult angling situations. The reader is again referred to the numerous books and references on the market that detail the specific use and techniques associated with each cast. Now let's take a closer look at two of these casts that have widespread applicability in fly-angling— the roll and curve casts. Since these two casts do not involve a whole new set of motions on the part of the angler, the physics of these casts is similar, with minor variations, to the above discussion.

The roll cast is particularly valuable when there is dense vegetation or trees behind the angler that would interfere with the back cast. Therefore, the roll cast incorporates only a forward motion to the rod, but with different timing to the application of the force by the angler. At the beginning of the cast, the rod is parallel to the water surface, and what may seem paradoxical at first is that the line is already on the water. The angler then lifts the rod slowly through an angle of 90 degrees so that the rod tip is now pointing straight up. This lifting of the rod slides the line to the angler. The line must come to a complete stop; otherwise, the application of the force on the forward stroke will go somewhat to stopping the line instead of propelling the line forward. At this stage, the surface tension, a property of water in which the water molecules cling together to form a thin, elastic film, comes into play with regard to making the cast. The surface tension, which results from the attractive force of water molecules for each other, causes the fly line to remain stationary within the surface film of the water. Fly anglers like to refer to this phenomenon as the water "grabbing" the line. Now the angler is poised to apply the force to the line. This is accomplished when the angler accelerates his forearm in a karate-chop manner and stops the casting stroke when the rod is parallel to the water surface. As energy is imparted to the line from the accelerated movement of the rod, the line that was initially stationary on the water surface rolls out in the form of a traveling closed loop until the line straightens out. Timing is critical at the end of the cast. If the angler stops the stroke too high above the surface, the line will roll out into the air instead of on the water surface. Stopping too low with rod tip pointed downward results in the line being driven into the water. I cannot overemphasize the fundamental principle that the line and fly go in the direction of the application of the force. Since the angler has a shorter accelerating path than in the case discussed above, the rod must be accelerated quickly to break the surface tension of the water and to impart the maximum energy to the line. As with the scenario presented before, the nature and material of the rod are critical to this cast. Long rods also aid in achieving distance during the roll cast, since the tip will travel a greater distance than with short rods. In addition, rods that are relatively stiff minimize unwanted vibrations at the end of the casting stroke when the angler has to stop abruptly.

Fly anglers often encounter some unique challenges with regard to casting to tight spots or difficult locations. Obviously, this is one of the intrinsic appeals of fly-fishing. The cast that most competent anglers should master to meet these situations is the curve cast. As the name implies, the line, particularly the end portion, will curve or hook to either the right or left of its original path. This cast will allow the angler to tuck the fly back under vegetative overhangs where trout reside seeking protective cover, position the fly around an in-stream obstacle such as a rock, and increase the length of drift of the fly on the water.

Let's see how the line and fly can curve to the left from a right-hander's perspective. The same principles also pertain to a right-curve cast. Many instructors tell their pupils to initiate this cast using a side-arm motion to the casting stroke and to slightly "overpower" the cast with a sharp, precise stroke. The only variation to the casting mechanics that we discussed above is the plane in which the angler accelerates and stops the rod. The rod is moved in the horizontal plane instead of the vertical plane. While the term *overpower* is applied incorrectly in describing the mechanics of the cast, the important factor is where the angler stops the acceleration stroke and the direction the rod tip points. In this case the rod tip is pointing slightly to the left. As noted above, an unfurling line will encounter air resistance that will not only decrease the line speed but also, in the case of this cast, change its direction. This results because the air resistance is an opposing force to the initial direction of the fly line (fig. 11).

Though we will deal with this in more detail in later sections, this resistance to motion is commonly referred to as *drag*. It causes the end portion of the line to have a pronounced hook to the left. The opposing effect of air resistance also increases with the speed of an object. Recall from our discussion of fly-line speed that the tip of the line speeds up as the line unrolls from the tip of the rod. Therefore we would expect the tip portion of the line to have the most pronounced curvature. In addition, the air resistance acting on the fly adds a curvature component to the overall displacement of the line. Bulky flies with a large surface area are aerodynamically inefficient and thus enhance the degree of fly-line curvature due to increased air resistance.

While I suppose Isaac Newton was probably never an avid fly angler, I am sure that he would be pleased to see that his second law of motion has such an influence on the discipline of fly casting. If you keep in mind the relatively basic physics principles applicable to casting and incorporate these principles in casting, your skills will improve considerably. Theory is fine, but fly anglers like to experiment—practice casting.

FIG. 11. Curve cast in response to air resistance

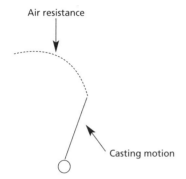

Air resistance

Casting motion

Technical Focus

1. In the photographic and quantitative analysis by Mosser and Buchman (1980) the energy from the casting motion was approximately four times greater than from the unbending of the rod. Significant stored energy exchange takes place only at the start and end of the casting stroke. During most of the casting stroke, while the caster is imparting energy to the line, the stored energy component is relatively constant. They also showed that there is a loss of energy during the reverse bend in the rod that has occurred due to the fundamental frequency of the rod. Some of the stored energy has gone into causing the tip of the rod to wiggle and consequently is not transferred to the line. The above discussion can be summarized by the following simple energy balance relationship

$$E_f = E_c + E_b - E_v$$

where E_f is the energy supplied to the fly line, E_c equals energy supplied by the casting motion, E_b is the energy supplied by the unbending of the rod, and E_v is the energy lost due to vibration. The left-hand term of the above equation can be expressed in terms of kinetic energy (line speed) and the right-hand terms as the amount of work necessary to generate the line speed.

$$\frac{mv^2}{2} = F_c d_1 + F_b d_2 - F_v d_3$$

The speed of the line is equal to the force applied by the caster to the line as the rod is moved through the casting distance, plus the force from the unbending of the rod over its spring distance, minus the force from unbending over the vibration distance.

2. The changing velocity $v(t)$ of the fly line as a function of time can be expressed in the following relationship

$$v(t) = [mv^2/m(t)]^{1/2}$$

where m and v are initial mass and velocity of the line, and mt is the changing mass of the unfurling fly line. Consider the bracketed terms. The numerator is the initial kinetic energy of the line, and the denominator is the changing mass as a function of time of the top portion of the line. Note that, as the denominator decreases due to the line unfurling but the numerator remains constant, the velocity of the line must increase.

FOUR

The Fly Angler's Environment

INTEREST IN FLY-FISHING HAS INCREASED SIGNIFicantly over the last decade, spurred on in part by affordable and relatively user-friendly equipment, increased exposure both in the print and visual mediums, and changes in attitudes regarding the social nature of the sport. Recent surveys have estimated the number of fly anglers in the United States at over 7 million, with females composing approximately 25 percent of this group. But this surge in popularity has not been without its downside. Local, easily accessible streams have become overcrowded and overexploited. Streams that were once held in public trust now have become privatized due to profit incentives and weariness over angling disputes. The seventeenth-century angler of Izaak Walton's time would have been totally dismayed by the current state of some of our most popular streams that have been all too overpromoted in magazines and books. For example, every year some 140,000 anglers fish the waters of the Madison River that flows through Montana (Monaghan 2002). The quest for solitude in relatively quiet, remote locations becomes of paramount importance to the dedicated fly angler. We want our "secret spot" or "honey hole" that provides us with both an aesthetically appealing location and a satisfying angling experience. But how can we locate these sites? How do we find our way there and back? A necessary tool to understand the lay of the land is a topographic map, which describes the physical features and nature of the land surface. Once the angler becomes familiar with the layout and symbols used on these maps, it will be relatively easy to locate various aquatic environments, like mountain streams, waterfalls, alpine lakes, and rapids. Planning that next fishing trip will no longer be a chore but part of the adventure and pleasure.

The U.S. Geological Survey prints the majority of topographic maps in the form of quadrangle charts. A quadrangle is a rectangular section of the earth's surface that is bounded by latitude and longitude coordinates (fig. 12). It may be a bit presumptuous on my part, but let's review some basic geographic principles. Latitude lines are parallel to the earth's equator (o degrees latitude) and measure distance north and south of this location. Longitude lines are oriented north-south and measure distance east and west of the prime meridian (o degrees longitude). A common form of the topographical quadrangle is the 15-minute series. Here the term *minute* does not refer to a unit of time but to measurement. Latitude and longitude measurements are expressed in degrees, minutes, and seconds. A minute is a subset of a degree, and correspondingly a second is a subset of a minute: 1 degree = 60 minutes, and 1 minute = 60 seconds. How would you determine, for example, the distance of a 15-minute quadrangle? A little arithmetic conversion is necessary to answer this question: 1 minute of latitude = 1.18 statute miles. Therefore, a 15-minute quadrangle covers approximately 18 miles in the north-south direction.

The direction of true north is toward the top of the map. If the angler is to use a compass to navigate, he should be aware that compasses point to the magnetic north as opposed to the geographic North Pole. The magnetic north pole is located just west of Hudson Bay in Canada. The angular difference between the direction of true north and magnetic north is known as the *magnetic declination.* It is expressed diagrammatically at the bottom of the topographic map, and it is easily interpreted with a little study.

A topographic map is simply a representation of a much larger portion of the earth's surface. Each linear distance on the earth's surface is represented by a much shorter distance on the map. The ratio between the map distance and the corresponding actual distance is the map scale. In the case of a topo-

THE SCIENCE OF FLY-FISHING

FIG. 12. Topographic map

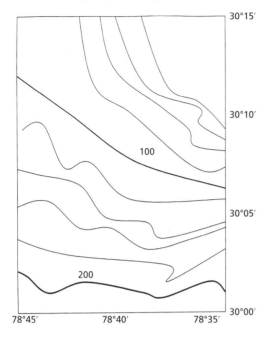

graphic map with a scale of 1:24,000, one unit (centimeter, inch) on a map is equivalent to 24,000 of the same units on land. Other common map scales are 1:62,500 and 1:250,000. It is definitely awkward for the angler to think of traveling a certain number of inches on the land. For a map with a 1:24,000 scale, a more meaningful representation to bear in mind is that one map inch equals 2,000 feet. In addition, three graphical scales, marked in units of miles, feet, and kilometers, are also printed on the bottom of the map. The angler can simply measure the distance between any two points on the map and, with the aid of the graphical scales, determine the actual distance.

Topographic maps are two-dimensional models of a three-dimensional surface. Though we have seen how horizontal distance is represented, what about elevation? This dimension is represented through the use of contour lines. A contour line connects all points on the map having the same elevation. Notice on the map (fig. 12) that some of these contour lines, *index contours,* are darker, thicker, and numbered with regard to elevation. The *contour interval* is the numerical difference between adjacent contour lines on the map. This value is generally stated at the bottom of the map, below the graphical scales.

If a point lies on an index contour, its elevation is determined simply from reading the numerical value. If the point in question lies on a nonindex contour, its elevation can be determined by simply reading up or down from the nearest index contour and keeping in mind the contour interval value. Though two alpine lakes on a map may have the same elevation, the steepness of the terrain to reach these sites may be significantly different. This steepness or vertical gradient is defined as *relief*—the difference in elevation between two points on a map. A qualitative estimate of the relief is determined by viewing the spacing of the contour lines. Contour lines that are bunched together are indicative of a terrain with steep relief. In contrast, if the spacing between the contours is wide, the trail in this region would be a relatively easy hike.

The fly angler who is proficient in using a topographic map and a compass could easily find that remote mountain stream and the way back out of the wilderness. By employing the technology of the Global Positioning System (GPS), one could navigate with a greater degree of accuracy. Utilizing the positioning data from a minimum of three orbiting satellites, a very accurate ground location is easily available to the user. The technology has advanced so rapidly that many GPS units are portable, hand-held size, and affordable. The GPS units have a navigational screen that provides position, course, speed, and time, and there is a memory system to store and recall favorite locations. For the backcountry angler, a topographic map and a GPS unit are indispensable in locating and navigating to that remote angling site.

Though topographic maps may allow us to focus in on that trickle of water cascading down the side of the mountain, we need to broaden our perspective to larger topographic features and their role in aquatic communities. The nature of the stream flow, water chemistry, biological productivity, and the stream's suitability as a trout habitat are ultimately dependent upon its surroundings. This region is commonly referred to as a *watershed* or *drainage basin*. It is defined as the area that topographically contributes all the water to the streams that drain this basin. The shape of the basin can be viewed as bowl-shaped with the relatively high ridges known as *drainage divides* that separate adjacent basins, and the topographically low areas being the network of streams within the basin. Some researchers believe that the shape and topography of drainage basins have had an impact on the evolution of Pacific versus Atlantic salmon. Wild salmon on the West Coast are genetically programmed to migrate to the ocean immediately after emerging from the spawning sites. In contrast, the Atlantic salmon spend a minimum of one year in their natal river but commonly spend two to three years. The speculation is that, since the Pacific drainage basins have short, steep streams with large seasonal water fluctuations, salmon will take their chances in the ocean instead of the relatively harsh stream environment. In contrast, the geology of the eastern seaboard has resulted in streams that drain gentler slopes, so flows are slower and deeper and have more stable water levels. Thus, the Atlantic salmon are not prone to leave their freshwater habitats as opposed to their Pacific counterparts.

In most drainage basins the network of stream flow has a branching treelike pattern (fig. 13). This type of configuration is called *dendritic*—derived from the Greek word *dendron,* "tree." A hierarchical pattern of classification has been used to define this system. The smallest permanently flowing stream is termed *first order.* For example, the stream headwaters, which originate in topographic highs, are first-order in nature and may be too small to hold trout. Two first-order streams coalesce to form a second-order stream and so on to form the dendritic network. The result of this classification is that larger rivers have a higher order than smaller streams.

The use of the terms *creek, stream,* or *river* conjures up the image of flowing water, but the casual reader may be hard-pressed to differentiate among them. It becomes even more confusing when we add some regional names like brook (as

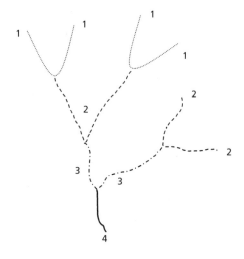

FIG. 13. Schematic diagram of dendritic drainage pattern

in brook trout), run, and kill. Present textbooks in hydrology do not set quantitative sizes and limits on these terms, nor do they help in differentiating among them. Let's try to clarify this situation by turning to an old, reliable source—the dictionary. The *American Heritage Dictionary* defines a stream as "a body of running water moving over the earth's surface in a channel or bed, as a brook, rivulet, or river." Additional searching yields that a river is "a large natural stream of water emptying into an ocean, lake, or other body of water and usually fed along its course by converging tributaries"; and a creek is "a small stream, often an intermittent tributary to a river." Well, it seems that a stream is the generic term for any confined freshwater flowing over the ground and that creeks and rivers are essentially differentiated by their size—small and big, respectively. However, the dictionary and other sources were of no help in delineating quantitatively when the transition occurs between creek and river. The term *run*, which is applied to some mountain streams in Virginia, turns out to be comparable in size to a creek. As pointed out by Nick Karas in his fine book *Brook Trout* (1997), the term *brook* comes from Old English—literally meaning small stream. The first Pilgrims who settled around Plymouth proceeded to name every river, stream, or creek a brook. The term *kill* that is often used in Delaware and New York state is even more obtuse, in that the dictionary defines it as being synonymous with a creek, river, or stream. An "overkill" (pun intended) situation might exist with the naming of the Battenkill River, a well-known trout stream that flows through parts of Vermont and New York.

In our quest for finding that ideal trout stream, Christopher Camuto probably best expresses our feelings when he writes, "Fly-fishing requires good taste in rivers because trout have good taste in rivers" (1988, 50). But ever wonder why some trout streams are more productive and healthy than comparable streams? The climate and geology that dominate within a watershed determine a number of physical characteristics of a river, such as amount of water transported, flow patterns, substrate composition, and shape of channel. These attributes viewed as a composite system strongly impact and influence the aquatic life in a river. It is therefore important to understand a fundamental natural phenomenon at work in the entire watershed—the hydrologic cycle. A cycle is a sequence of events that occur regularly. All cycles can be characterized by the following components: the matter or energy being transferred is occurring in a series of discrete events, the amount of matter or energy being transferred can be quantified, and cycles occur over characteristic space and time scales.

The water cycle involves the transfer of water in its various forms of liquid, vapor, and solid through the atmosphere, hydrosphere (ocean, rivers, groundwater), and biosphere. Energy from the sun evaporates water from the ocean. As this water vapor ascends into the atmosphere, it cools and condenses, forming cloud droplets. The precipitation falling from these clouds either is cycled directly back to the ocean or falls on land. The process of evaporation from lakes and streams and of transpiration by plants cycles water vapor back to the atmosphere. The remaining water returns to the ocean through the conduits of streams, groundwater flow, and runoff. Conceptually this cycle can be viewed as a series of storage places and transfer processes. If one of the transfer processes, like precipitation, is adversely affected by prolonged drought, then the water storage in the lakes and streams will decrease, reflecting a decrease in the inputs of runoff and groundwater. Though climate is the determining factor with regard to the amount of precipitation received by a watershed, the ultimate quantity and quality of water entering a stream is determined by the geology and biology of the surrounding landscape. The relative profusion of vegetation and the richness and thickness of soils within a watershed influence both the amount of sediment washed into the stream and the amount of water delivered to the stream after a rainfall event. Though the amount of precipitation falling upon the watershed may be significant, the buffering effects of leaf litter, mature tree stands, and riparian vegetation will result in streams running clear and steady. Thick, rich soils allow for significant infiltration of precipitation into the subsurface reservoir, thereby controlling the amount of surface runoff. Correspondingly, in areas of thin, poor soils and little vegetative cover, streams are subject to wide swings in current flow as literally sheets of water enter unimpeded into the stream channel.

As we have just learned, the composite effects of climate, geology, and the nature of the watershed ultimately determine the amount of water flowing within a stream channel. Suitable trout habitat is dependent upon adequate water flow. A segment of a channel may be inhabitable during low flow periods but can become an excellent habitat for spawning females during high flows. A stream's *discharge* is defined as the volume of water flowing past a given location on the stream channel per unit of time, usually measured in cubic feet per second. Monthly flows, annual peaks in flow, and frequency and magnitude of flood events are discharge statistics computed from stream-gauge or water surface elevation (stage) data. Hydrologists have developed relationships linking stage to discharge, but it is beyond the intent of this book to pursue this topic in additional detail. Suffice it to say that the

United States Geological Survey maintains a network of sites throughout the country that can provide long-term records of stream discharge. A stream's discharge can change significantly over time, reflecting significant precipitation events, wet seasons, or drought periods. During a sudden intense thunderstorm, stream discharge may increase dramatically, particularly in streams with small cross-sectional areas. From the angler's perspective, this may mean a torrent of water being funneled into small channels. The resultant increase in current speed may make fly-fishing not only impractical but dangerous if the angler is wading the stream. It is important to note that higher-order streams in the watershed will generally have the highest speeds, since these are final depositories for water flow from the lower-order tributaries. What fly angler hasn't experienced the disappointment of seeing that once deep, cold pool shrink to the size of a puddle during a long, hot summer? Disruptions in the hydrological cycle due to drought conditions can send both fish and angler scurrying about in search of new watering holes.

Since stream discharge is critical to the survival of all salmonid species, it is often the key variable in many stream restoration projects. In the event that gauge data is not available for a particular stream, discharge can be determined by measuring the average stream velocity and the cross-sectional area (width times depth) of the stream channel. The discharge is simply equal to the product of velocity multiplied by the area. The empirical data from which velocity is determined can be collected with the aid of a current meter—similar to those that determine wind speed—measuring the flow at a particular point in the stream. Though you may want to involve personnel from a local college science department to aid in these measurements, a crude, but fun, estimation can be made by releasing a float (a fishing bobber will do) upstream a predetermined distance and measuring the time it takes for the float to cover this distance. The velocity is then determined by dividing the distance by the time.

The velocity of water in a stream is the result of two opposing forces—gravity and friction. Obviously, the force of gravity is the reason that water flows downstream, or from higher to lower elevations. Since gravity is a vertically directed force, its influence increases with the slope or steepness of the channel. Friction is always an impediment to motion, resulting in a decrease in current flow. Friction results as moving water comes into contact with the streambed, bottom obstructions, and the sides of the stream channel. The highest velocities are found where friction is least, generally at or near the water surface and near the center of the channel. For example, consider two streams with the same channel slope but differing in depth. The deeper river will have a greater velocity than the shallower river, since the dissipative influence of the bottom is minimized in the deep channel. However, in both cases, stream velocity decreases as a function of depth. The exact nature of the velocity profile (linear, logarithmic) or how current speed changes with depth depends upon a myriad of factors including the nature of the stream bottom and size of obstacles interfering with the flow. Since the spawning of salmonids occurs on gravel streambeds and the incubation of these eggs depends upon adequate water flow, salmonids are particularly sensitive to changes in current velocity. Studies of rainbow trout in western rivers have shown that, though these fish spawned in velocities ranging from 0.8 to 3.2 ft/sec, they had a preferred range of 1.6 to 3.0 ft/sec. A fly angler fishing a deep, swift-flowing river with a weighted nymph should also be aware of the effect of the current on the fly line. The portion of the line on the surface will be dragged along by the fast-flowing surface water, while, in contrast, the nymph will sink to a depth of decreased flow. The difference in the current flow with depth necessitates an on-stream adjustment by the angler. To compensate for the unnatural drag on the fly line, the angler should reposition (mend) the line so that a more natural drift is obtained.

A continuous record of discharge plotted against time is called a *hydrograph* (fig. 14). A hydrograph has a number of characteristics that reflect the pathways and rapidity with which precipitation inputs reach the stream. *Baseflow* represents groundwater input to the river. Many spring creeks depend upon this component to maintain an adequate discharge and current flow for its inhabitants. Rainstorms result in an increase above baseflow—storm runoff. The shape and timing of this rising limb of the hydrograph is dependent upon the nature of the rain event, morphology of the basin, vegetation, and soil characteristics. For example, a basin with a large storage capacity, absorptive surface, and dense vegetation will have a lower discharge peak than a corresponding basin that has impermeable soils and sparse vegetation. Significant runoff within the basin causes a rapid and pronounced increase in stream discharge and may also result in significant soil erosion within the basin. The duration of the peak discharge may vary from a few minutes for a small mountain creek to days for a large river. This is due to the variations in the amount and duration of precipitation received within a basin and the variable response of the tributaries to the precipitation input. The descending branch (recession limb) of the hydrograph describes the return to baseflow conditions and is generally more gradual and not as abrupt as the ascending branch.

FIG. 14. Schematic diagram of a hydrograph

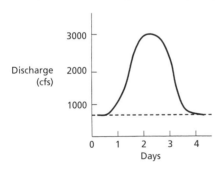

Long-term stream-flow data can be analyzed to generate statistics that have application in design engineering, flood control, and stream restoration projects. One example of this type of analysis is estimation of the probability of a particular discharge event occurring over a specific time frame—the proverbial 1-in-100-year flood of a given magnitude. The period between two discharges of a particular magnitude recurring is then 100 years. The probability (*P*) of a discharge event can be expressed as

$$P = 1/T$$

where *T* is the recurrence interval. Thus a 1-in-100-year flood has a probability of 0.01 (1 percent). Let's work through an example that will hopefully clarify this topic. Consider a stream that has an annual maximum discharge of 5,000 cubic feet per second and the recurrence interval for this event is 25 years; thus, the probability is 0.04, or 4 percent. Are you still with me? Let's proceed! It should be emphasized that the discharge is not one that occurs like clockwork, every 25 years; it is a discharge that has a 4 percent probability of occurring every year. If the discharge of 5,000 cubic feet per second occurred this year, there is still a 4 percent chance that another discharge of the same magnitude will occur the following year. Now the argument gets a bit more esoteric, but you will soon see its relevance. With the magic of some statistical principles, we could determine the probability of 5,000 cubic feet per second being equaled or exceeded in two *consecutive* years.

$$P[2] = P \times P = 0.04 \times 0.04 = 0.0016 \text{ or } 0.016\%$$

Now, if an engineer has designed and installed an in-stream structure capable of holding up to this discharge, then the probability of that event being equaled or exceeded during both years is relatively small; hence, very minimal risk. If a log dam was placed in a stream to form an upstream pool for improved trout habitat, then there is a very good chance that this restoration project would still be around over this two-year period if discharges never exceeded 5,000 cubic feet per second. Similar to assessing one's risk tolerance with regard to financial investing, the above analysis is simply to make one aware that the risk of implementing in-stream improvements can and should be determined before any actual labor is expended on the project.

As we have discussed, all water enters the land component of the hydrologic cycle as precipitation. Thus, in order to assess and forecast hydrologic response within a watershed, we need to look at the temporal and spatial variations of precipitation. Since maximum snowmelt rates are much lower than maximum rainfall rates, extreme values of rainfall in amount and duration are of greater interest in flood frequency analysis. Rainfall intensity is defined as the amount of rainfall divided by its duration. Intense rainfall, like the proverbial "cloudburst," may lead to very high discharges, significant stream erosion, trout habitat alteration, and significant sediment deposition.

What are the factors that allow some clouds to produce a drizzle as compared to those clouds that yield copious amounts of rainfall? Though the physics of rain production within the cloud is quite complex, three cloud variables stand out in importance—the cloud's water content, cloud thickness, and the updrafts within the cloud. Those clouds that have a high water density are very likely to produce significant rainfall amounts as a result of in-cloud processes that enhance droplet size. Relatively thin stratus clouds, the kind that give us those gray, overcast days, may be able to produce only a small amount of rain. In contrast, the towering cumulonimbus cloud, more commonly known as a thunderstorm, in some cases attains heights of over 50,000 feet and may yield prodigious amounts of rainfall. While the updrafts are relatively weak in stratus clouds, the vertical motion in a thunderstorm may reach speeds of over 75 miles per hour. These intense updrafts "power" the thunderstorm as a result of the release of energy from the condensing water vapor in the rising air.

Thunderstorms that have all the above ingredients, which are necessary to produce exceptional amounts of precipitation, are called *severe thunderstorms* and may result in flash floods within the watershed. A particularly unique example of a severe thunderstorm is a *supercell storm*—an enormous storm and one of exceptional intensity that may persist for hours. One such storm occurred on July 31, 1976, in Big Thompson

Canyon, Colorado. During a one-hour period, rainfall totals reached 7.5 inches and in some locales total storm rainfall equaled 10.6 inches. This high rainfall intensity, coupled with the steep terrain of the canyon, spawned a flash flood with an initial wall of water reaching 20 feet in height. The flood resulted in significant geomorphic changes within the canyon's watershed, including river-channel scouring, aquatic habitat alteration and destruction, and massive amounts of fine sediments being deposited on channel bars and on the floodplain.

More recently, on June 27, 1995, a long-lived storm near the Blue Ridge Mountains of Virginia produced record flooding in the Rapidan River basin. This storm ranks as one of the most intense in the central Appalachian region in terms of hydrologic and geomorphic impacts. Total rainfall accumulations for the storm exceeded 24 inches for a six-hour period. The peak flood discharge on the Rapidan River was estimated at 100,000 cubic feet per second over a drainage area of 100 square miles. For comparison purposes, the Nile River has an average *monthly* discharge of 98,500 cubic feet per second with a drainage area of approximately 1 million square miles. In both of these, and other documented cases, orographic effects significantly contributed to the intensity of the storms. The main effect induced by the topography is the generation of strong upslope winds, which contribute copious amounts of water vapor to fuel the storm. Whenever a river and its watershed experience catastrophic rainfalls and flooding, it may take years to decades for the environment to return to its prestorm state. Life within the river is adversely affected as fish community structure is altered, water quality declines, habitats are altered, and food chains are disrupted. The healing process cannot be fast enough for the angler waiting to return to the river.

If the stream discharge from a nasty thunderstorm doesn't wipe out a favorite trout stream, there is another thunderstorm-related phenomenon that has a more direct impact on the fly angler—lightning. Lightning is also a type of discharge but is electrical in nature. It is essentially a giant spark that occurs in thunderstorms. Lightning may occur within a cloud, from cloud to cloud, and from a cloud to the ground. Most of the lightning bolts occur within a cloud, with only 20 percent of the discharges occurring between the ground and the cloud. Since a lightning stroke may involve a current of 100,000 amperes, which can result in electrocution, let's focus on the cloud-to-ground lightning. The potential for an electrical discharge exists when two objects have different electrical charges. A neutral object becomes negatively charged when it gains electrons and positively charged when it loses electrons. The objects become ionized. Though there is still debate among atmospheric scientists about how clouds become electrified, measurements have shown that the base of the cloud is negatively charged. This negatively charged bottom of the cloud induces a strong positive charge on the ground. The difference in charges between the cloud and the ground is called the electrical potential. Even though unlike electrical charges attract one another, a flow of current does not occur initially, because air is a good electrical insulator. It simply doesn't like to transport these charges. As the electrical potential increases and reaches a critical value (1 million volts per yard), the insulating properties of air are overcome, an electrical current flows, and lightning occurs. The positive charges on the ground tend to be concentrated on tall objects like trees, buildings, and fly rods. Since the positive-charge concentration will be maximum at the rod tip, this increases the probability that lightning will strike the tip and travel down the rod and into you. That 9-foot graphite fly rod that you are flailing about in pursuit of your prey becomes the proverbial lightning rod in "attracting" lightning.

Obviously safety takes priority over catching that trophy trout (it will still be there when you return). Put down that rod and exit the water as quickly as possible. Even though the lightning bolt may not strike you directly, water as opposed to air is a good conductor of electricity. Standing in an open stream (rubber waders offer no protection) is inviting electrical mayhem. In addition, if you are hiking up a mountain trail to a remote alpine lake, then you may be particularly vulnerable to being struck by lightning. Not only may you be above the tree line—hence the tallest object around—but also climatological studies have shown that the frequency of thunderstorms increases with elevation. The key is always to seek appropriate shelter such as a house, barn, or car, but remember: do not sit under that apple tree!

FIVE

Streams: Characteristics and Morphology

WHILE THE PREVIOUS CHAPTER DISCUSSED THE importance of the watershed on streams, we will now try to dissect the nature of streams and their relationship to their major inhabitants—the fish. Whether it is a river, creek, stream, or designated by another name, humans have always been fascinated with moving water. Native Americans often attached a mystical significance to their local streams. These waters provided them with food and a means of transportation, and its creatures often served as religious spirits. Whole native cultures, particularly of the Northwest, developed and thrived around water. Ceremonies and religious events were often tied to the seasonal arrival of the salmon.

Numerous writers have attempted to explain this human attraction to water. Thoreau said that a man went fishing all of his life without ever realizing that it was not the fish he was after. Thoreau was probably justified in this observation, as the modern-day fly angler is a divided person: interested in catching that wild, elusive trout but just as content being hip-deep in a clear, cold stream losing himself in nature. Though streams play a critical role in shaping the land through which they flow, they are conduits for the movement of both humans and animals and support diverse aquatic and riparian (stream-side) ecosystems that, in terms of biodiversity, are some of the richest on Earth. From a scientific perspective, streams have been actively studied for more than two centuries. Some of this research has included assessing the role of physical and chemical characteristics of a stream on its biota, how flowing water forms and alters habitat, and the adaptation of stream dwellers to varying stream environments. Christopher Hunter, in *Better Trout Habitat* (1991) probably summarizes our intense feeling about streams when he states, "Each stream is a whole greater than the sum of its geologic, hydrologic, and biologic parts. And wild trout are the product of this complex interaction" (11).

One of the main characteristics differentiating lowland streams from mountain streams is the gradient. The gradient of a stream/river channel is a change in its elevation along its horizontal course of flow. The gradient of a river channel may be represented by a longitudinal profile—a topographical profile along the length of the channel. The majority of streams and rivers exhibit a downstream decrease in gradient along their length. The steepest slopes are generally found in the headwaters, with a corresponding decrease in slope toward the mouth of the river. As water flows downward from higher elevations, it drops with considerable speed and over time erodes its way to the bedrock. The ability of a stream to erode depends on its energy, which is proportional to both its velocity and discharge. A swift, high-volume discharge can move boulders, in addition to carrying a large load of sediment. All of this change in the geomorphology of the stream channel has a profound effect on the suitability of a particular stream for trout.

In viewing different types of stream channels and their respective gradients, we introduce the term stream *reach*—relatively homogenous associations of topographic features and channel geomorphic units that distinguish them from other units. Stream reaches, reflecting differences in elevation, climate, and substrate composition, result in a great diversity of aquatic biota. Though research has classified eight distinct reaches, we will simplify the classification to four reaches as it pertains to trout habitat:

1. CASCADE REACH: steepest channel (slope of 8% to 30%), with water tumbling over and around boulders and large wood debris (logs, limbs, root wads greater than 3 inches in diameter), abundant waterfalls, only a few small pockets of reduced velocity flow to harbor trout;

2. STEP-POOL REACH: channels are characterized by a regular downstream alternation of steps composed of clasts (rock fragments), large woody debris or bedrock, and plunge pools. Scouring as water plunges vertically over an obstacle forms these pools. A high gradient (4% to 8%) reach with a staircase profile (fig. 15).

FIG. 15. Profile of stream reaches

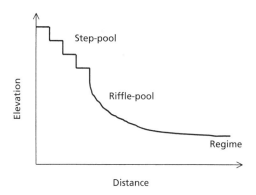

3. RIFFLE-POOL REACH: very prevalent in alluvial valleys of low to moderate gradient (0.1% to 2%). Unlike the cascade and step-pool reaches that are straight, the channel shape is often sinuous and contains alternating sequence of riffles (fast and shallow water moving over a cobble/gravel substrate) and pools composed of cobble and gravel substrate. The types of pools found here may differ in their morphology from plunge pools; for example, dammed pools form when debris spanning a channel causes water to collect upstream of the obstacle. In contrast, if a root wad or fallen tree channels the flow along its length, then a lateral scour pool may form. A backwater or eddy pool can be formed behind debris and other obstacles located in the channel margin. Each of these pools is unique with regard to water flow, sediment, and nutrient retention. Research has shown that the pool volume, hence the number of trout it can hold, is inversely related to stream gradient and directly related to the amount of large woody debris in the stream.

4. REGIME REACH: consists of low gradient (< 0.1%), meandering channels with predominantly sand substrate, although may have gravel and pebble substrate.

As stated above, the riffle-pool and regime reaches have a more sinuous course than either the cascade or step-pool reaches, though straight-as-an-arrow channels are quite uncommon in the natural world. The most commonly used measure of channel curvature (fig. 16) is the sinuosity index (SI)—the channel length divided by the down valley length. Streams with an SI value of less than 1.5 are considered *sinuous*. Those greater than 1.5 are considered *meandering*. In general, fisheries biologists have shown that sinuous/meandering channels are generally more suitable for trout than straight channels because of their potential to form suitable habitats. For example, the current flow though a meandering channel causes predictable regions of erosion and deposition. The region of maximum velocity and the deepest part of the channel, or *thalweg,* lie closest to the outside portion of each bend and subsequently cross over downstream to the other bank. In these meandering channels, deep pools characterize the outer bend of the channel and the inner portion is characterized by gravel point bars (fig. 17). The natural flow processes create pools with undercut banks on the outside bends of streams and also lead to the creation of eddies and backwaters, all of which are prime trout habitat. Riffles normally form as the thalweg crosses from one pool to another pool on the opposite bank.

The term *freestone* refers to any flowing water that has a bottom composed of rock that may range in size from boulders to gravel. Generally, though not entirely limited to this classification, most freestone streams originate in mountainous terrain. Cascade, step-pool, and riffle-pool reaches are freestone flows. Watershed runoff is often the main or only source of water for these flows. Hence, freestone streams may exhibit large seasonal variations in discharge. During late winter and spring runoff, these streams are fast and strong, resulting in significant bank erosion, with the sediments being transported downstream. However, if the stream has a considerable amount of stable woody debris, sediment stored in the low-

FIG. 16. Measurement of the sinuosity of a stream channel

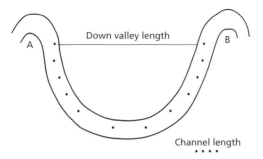

velocity zone of the debris dam has a larger residence time than it would likely have in a uniform-gradient channel. This increase in substrate stability and heterogeneity provides more diverse habitat for aquatic organisms. In the summer and fall, water levels generally drop, exposing numerous gravel bars along their edges. Algae attached to the channel bottom and nonvascular plants such as moss and lichens constitute most of the aquatic vegetation in freestone flows. Though this slippery vegetation may be a nuisance to the wading angler, these organisms are uniquely adapted to the nature of the substrate, the seasonal variability in discharge, and the inconsistent nutrient loadings from the watershed. With regard to understanding the biota within a freestone environment, Ellen Wohl, a noted expert on mountain streams, maintains that the viewer must assume a multidimensional perspective. Four basic dimensions are considered: lateral (across the stream channel), vertical, longitudinal, and temporal. Changes and

FIG. 17. Meandering flow pattern and stream features

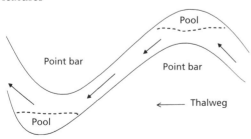

exchange at different spatial and temporal scales ultimately determine the nature and composition of a river ecosystem. For example in the longitudinal dimension, organic matter (leaf litter, decaying wood) stored in a quiet pool of a riffle-pool reach may be swept downstream during periods of high discharge and thus alter the diversity of the aquatic community. Vertical discharge may occur when sand and silt particles stored in a stream reach are brought into suspension during periods of high discharge, resulting in an alteration of stream habitats. You may be scratching your head at this time, wondering how this discussion relates to trout in a stream. Remember the abundance and vitality of a trout population reflect the geological and physical forces that shaped their stream. Many fly anglers attach great importance to catching fish in their native settings. They go to great lengths to go to places where the fish are a product of their environment.

Adjacent to stream channels are the zones of riparian vegetation. Depending upon geographical location, the nature of the vegetation with regard to specific species is quite variable, essentially reflecting the regional climate. The one common denominator that is characteristic of vegetation found in free-stone environments is its tolerance for floods and disturbances along the floodplain. In mountainous regions, elevation is a major factor determining climate and hence the nature of the riparian vegetation. Hiking up alongside your favorite mountain stream, you would notice a distinct change in vegetation from the lower stream reaches to the headwaters. Regardless of the type of vegetation that borders the stream, its importance with regard to influencing water quantity and quality cannot be minimized. Riparian vegetation decreases the volume of overland flow, limits streamside erosion, and influences both soil and water chemistry.

In contrast to mountain freestone streams, *spring creeks* generally have gentle gradients and tend to exhibit a considerable degree of sinuosity. Both the riffle-pool and regime reaches can be found along the length of these creeks. The main source of water is from underground flow, such as subsurface springs. Exchanges between groundwater and stream may impact water chemistry, temperature, and volume of flow. In some streams approximately 80 percent of the total annual discharge is derived from these underground sources at a relatively constant rate throughout the year. The low contribution from runoff results in a relatively stable hydrologic regime that has infrequent floods or droughts. This spring-fed water has a constant temperature throughout the year that results in both high daily and seasonal thermal stability. While summer water temperatures in small freestone pools may rise to lethal levels for trout, this is generally not a problem in spring creek pools. A unique variation of the spring creek mode is the limestone stream, including the famous trout chalk streams of England. A major factor that controls the dynamics and chemistry of these streams is the underlying calcareous bedrock. Chalk streams typically have low gradients due to this underlying geology. The combination of limited relief and hydrologic stability results in a low-energy environment, and consequently pool-riffle development is often absent. Water flowing over this bedrock results in dissolution of the calcareous material and high dissolved mineral concentrations. While sections of the stream substrate will have extensive beds of gravel and cobble, stream bank and other in-stream environments will have a sand and silt substrate. This substrate provides a base for aquatic vegetation, particularly macrophytes (characterized by having roots and differentiated tissue), to take hold. Some of these plants grow along the water's edge; others, called emergers, grow out of the water. Whether

TABLE 2. Properties of freestone streams versus spring creeks

Type	Freestone Stream	Spring Creek
Reaches	Cascade, step-pool, riffle-pool	Regime
Water	Runoff	Underground
Discharge	Seasonal	Constant
Aquatic plants	Attached algae, moss	Rooted plants
Riparian veg	Trees (conifers and deciduous)	Shrubs, trees
Trout	brook, brown, rainbow	Brown, rainbow

it is a spring creek, limestone, or chalk stream, many of these streams meander through meadows or agricultural land. The nature of the riparian vegetation depends to a certain extent upon the degree of human influence. Left undisturbed, streamside trees, chiefly alders and willows, and bushes will predominate. Where grazing is minimal, a diversity of vegetation will flourish in the silty margins of the stream. Table 2 summarizes the differences that we have discussed between freestone streams and spring creeks.

The chemical and physical characteristics, including velocity, magnitude and frequency of discharge, sediment loads, dissolved substance, and substrate grain size, of both freestone streams and spring creeks are the environmental agents that control the abundance and diversity of aquatic organisms. For example, the composition of the substrate is critical with regard to insect production, protection, and suitability for spawning. With regard to the latter point, the majority of the salmonids require clean gravel- to cobble-sized particles for the deposition and survival of the eggs. If these substrate particles are surrounded or covered by sediment, trout reproduction is severely affected. Since trout integrate the environmental factors, what and how much enters a stream has a major impact on the survivability and vitality of trout. This will be a common theme throughout the remainder of this book.

The biological resources on which trout depend are the result of both autochthonous and allochthonous production. Though these terms may seem intimidating, never mind barely pronounceable, the following discussion will elucidate their relevance. *Autochthonous production* is the creation of living matter in the stream channel via photosynthesis. Now, this last term may be familiar from your high school biology class, but let's refresh your memory. In the photosynthetic process, organic matter (carbon-based compounds such as carbohydrates) is formed or synthesized from carbon dioxide and water, using light as an energy source. The major biological organisms responsible for this process are the aquatic plants found within the streams. Though the algae and mosses are the main photosynthetic agents in mountain streams, the high nutrient concentration, good light penetration, and stable discharge of spring creeks result in high autochthonous production. *Allochthonous production* depends upon particulate matter in the form of decaying organic matter (detritus) that enters the aquatic environment from outside the stream channel, generally in the form of leaf litter and decaying wood. The abundance of plant material and detritus supports a robust population of macro invertebrates. These organisms, which include aquatic insects, crustaceans, mollusks, leeches, and amphipods, are the dominant species within the aquatic environment, in some cases composing 98 percent of a stream's living matter. But in high-gradient, temperate streams, 90 percent of the bottom population is composed of aquatic insects that exhibit unique feeding strategies suitable to their environment. For example, shredders feed on nonwoody coarse particulate organic matter, such as leaves. Collectors feed on finer organic matter that they gather from the surface or filter from the current, and grazers scrape the biofilm assemblages (attached algae, bacteria, and fungi) that coat the in-stream gravel and rocks.

The unique physical and chemical environments of both mountain streams and spring creeks support a distinctive and diverse fish fauna. Obviously, from our sporting perspective, the Salmonidae family is well represented by trout and salmon. The number and size of salmonids in chalk streams is generally higher than in other lotic environments. The high biological productivity, thermal stability, and discharge stability provide a favorable environment for the growth of salmonids. In contrast, trout in small mountain streams usually grow more slowly than those in farm and country streams and rarely attain weights of more than 1 to 2 pounds. These high-altitude streams are not very fertile, so they produce considerably less food. Some streams display a longitudinal zonation of fish communities. For example, in some eastern streams brook trout dominate in step-pool reaches, and brown and rainbow trout are found in meandering reaches. In comparison, the low gradient of spring creeks and chalk streams is not conducive to this vertical zonation.

Our goal so far has been to demonstrate the interrelationship between widely varying spatial scales, and their subsequent physical and chemical characteristics, in relation to providing a suitable environment for trout. The approach is similar to that of Charles Frissell and colleagues, who proposed considering spatially nested levels of resolution (fig. 18) to characterize lotic form and process. We are working our way down this staircase of spatial environments, from a watershed totaling hundreds of square miles to microhabitats of about one square yard in size.

FIG. 18. Spatially nested levels of resolution (after Frissell et al. 1986)

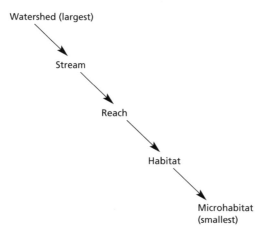

The flow of water or current is the defining characteristic of creeks, streams, and rivers. The speed of the current determines the size of particles that can be conveyed downstream and the degree the flow of water sculpts the stream's banks. The currents transport food to the waiting organisms and are essential in the removal of biotic waste products. As we will see in a later section, currents exert a direct physical force on organisms struggling to maintain their position in the flowing water.

For the beginning fly angler, attempting to decipher and analyze current flow within a stream can be intimidating, whether it be a large, swift-flowing river or a slow, meandering spring creek. The interpretation of the stream's structure becomes the angler's Rorschach test. Yet the angler must be able to observe, comprehend, and utilize what the river is telling him—what fly writers call "reading the water." Barry Lopez has articulated this idea: "That for an angler the highest and most treasured skill is not the catching of fish, but the reading of a river" (1989, 72). Philip Johnson continues along the same path: "There are all sorts of sound, pragmatic reasons for learning the language of streams. Still the deepest motivation may be the pleasure of simply observing and understanding the ebb and flow of a river and its chain of life" (1986, 35).

What does the angler look for upon encountering a river for the first time? Essentially, the observer is looking for *current breaks*—changes in the speed and/or direction of the current flow. These changes may be the result of substrate topography and composition, shape of the channel and its banks, and obstacles and obstructions. For example, a rough streambed creates more frictional resistance to flow than a smooth one. Boulders increase turbulence and resistance, so a current flows more slowly through a rough channel than a smooth one.

Trout in a stream intuitively understand the nuances of current flow, since ultimately their survival is dependent upon it. In order to be successful stream residents, trout must satisfy these needs: gas exchange, food, comfortable temperature, and protection. One of the prominent behavioral characteristics that researchers have noted of all salmonids is their need to establish and defend specific territories within a stream. A subset of this territory is what fly anglers refer to as "holding places" that allow trout to feed, rest, and escape from predators. Holding places become our microhabitats. How do these holding places meet the basic needs of the trout?

GAS EXCHANGE. Essential to the vital life functions of aquatic animals is the process of bringing oxygen into the body and eliminating carbon dioxide. Oxygen, which makes up about 21 percent of the total volume of dry air, dissolves into water from exchange with the atmosphere. As the fish faces into the water flow, it pumps the oxygen-laden water past its gill membranes and releases the water through rear-facing gill slits. The higher concentration of oxygen dissolved in the water causes oxygen to diffuse through the gill membranes into the fish. Correspondingly, the path for carbon dioxide is reversed—eliminated to the water. The anatomical configuration of the gill membranes is such that the direction of blood flow through the capillaries is opposite to that of the incoming water, thereby increasing transfer efficiency. During prolonged periods of very low stream discharge, oxygen concentrations can decrease to critically low values.

In small, unpolluted, turbulent streams, dissolved oxygen concentrations are near saturation and generally are not a limiting factor for the aquatic life in the stream. If biological or chemical processes create demand for more dissolved oxygen within the water column, diffusion of oxygen across the air-water interface maintains concentrations very near to equilibrium. In large rivers with their small surface-area-to-volume ratio and generally less turbulent flow, diffusion of oxygen plays a reduced role in the river's concentration. In these cases, biological activity may significantly influence the dissolved oxygen concentrations. The starting point is a photosynthetic by-product—oxygen produced by the plants. Within the stream community, the plants, animals, and bacteria are consuming oxygen but "exhaling" carbon dioxide as result of respiration. Streams and rivers that support abundant aquatic vegetation, like macrophytes, may experience large diurnal swings in the dissolved oxygen concentration—increasing during the day as the result of photosynthesis and decreasing at night due to respiration.

FOOD. Most fish are part of a hierarchical food pyramid in which the lower-level organisms supply the nutritional needs of the apex organisms. Each step along the food pyramid is referred to as a *trophic* level. Plants are first-level trophic organisms, and consumers occupy the higher trophic levels. Scientists generally define the amount of organisms within an environment by means of its *biomass*—the collective weight of the organisms per unit area. Within the structure of the food pyramid, the biomass decreases from the lowest to the highest trophic level.

To grow and reproduce, larger organisms such as trout need to consume a large amount of smaller organisms, such as insects, below them on the food pyramid. The feeding trout converts the organic matter of the insect into chemical energy. The transfer of energy from one trophic level to the next is an inefficient process. When the fish consumes the food, most of the energy released through metabolism is expended as kinetic energy or is used in the construction of bones and scales. Only a small fraction of the energy from the food is converted to mass of the organism. Studies have shown energy efficiencies in freshwater aquatic environments range from 5 to 20 percent. Let's see what this means to our stream-dwelling trout. Using 10 percent transfer efficiency, our trout would gain only one pound even though consuming ten pounds of organisms that occupy the trophic level below it. Given this inefficiency, the trout cannot expend more energy in catching its prey than it would gain by consuming it. Studies have shown that trout prefer to inhabit a portion of a stream where they can obtain food easily. Within these "feeding stations" a trout can dart out into the current, intercept its prey, and return to its location with a minimum expenditure of energy. With regard to water flow, these feeding stations are associated with two distinct regimes (fig. 19):

FIG. 19. Current changes and holding places for fish

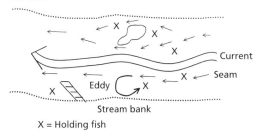

X = Holding fish

1. *Current seams:* a swift current flows next to a slow current. The trout spends a significant portion of its time in the

slower moving water, conserving its energy, only venturing into the fast flow to feed;

2. *Eddy:* a slow, circular flow of water moving counter to the main current flow. Food transported by the main current is essentially trapped within the eddy, providing easy access for the foraging trout.

PROTECTION. The long process of evolution has allowed salmonids, for the most part, to survive their natural predators. The majority of their predators are not found within the stream but are terrestrial (otters, bears) or avian (osprey, herons) in nature—coming from above. This inborn drive to survive has necessitated that trout and salmon seek in-stream safe havens. Biologists generally refer to this protective habitat as *cover*—an object-oriented site of sufficient depth. Rocks, logs, fallen trees, vegetation, and undercut banks may all provide suitable escape sites for the trout. Though these sites may also serve the purpose of feeding and resting stations, trout may seek the protection of these objects only when they feel threatened. The type of cover that the fish seek for protection tends to vary with the species in question. Studies have shown that cutthroat trout generally prefer the protection afforded by a blanket of fast, turbulent water. In contrast, brook trout seek calmer water and stream-bank cover. It is no surprise that there is a direct relationship between the availability and diversity of cover and the number of fish within a particular stream section.

TEMPERATURE. Though the topic of temperature is discussed in another chapter of this book, we will view it with regard to the location of trout in moving water. While the concept of territoriality is indeed pertinent to trout, these organisms may exhibit a wide spatial variation as a result of seasonal temperature changes. For example, during the winter and early spring, the generally high stream flows force trout to seek refuge in the deeper stream pockets. With spring in full bloom and water temperatures reaching above 50°F, temperature is not a limiting factor, and trout may be found anywhere within the stream—riffles, pools, flats. In some streams, summer may be the most stressful time for trout. With rising water temperatures and the subsequent decrease in dissolved oxygen content, trout will seek colder, more oxygenated water. These may be spring seeps or feeder streams that can locally lower the temperature. Trout may also even venture from their protective habitats into shallow riffles, where the turbulent water affords an increase in dissolved oxygen content.

Trout Holding Sites

This section will attempt to convey to the reader specific sites where the angler should consider casting a fly in the hope of encountering a lurking trout. There are obviously no guarantees, but if the angler keeps in mind that each site offers a particular advantage to the trout in satisfying its needs, the odds of locating a trout will increase.

ROCKS. As the current encounters it, a separation of flow occurs upstream of the rock. In this slower-moving water, trout may be found, waiting to move to either side to seize prey in the faster flow. A classic location is immediately behind the rock due to the markedly decreased flow and turbulence. This site affords maximum protection from the energy-sapping effects of the swift current.

DOWNED TREES. The advantage to the fish comes in the forms of both protection and breaks in the current. Studies have shown that the orientation of the trees in the stream, whether parallel or perpendicular to the current flow, is not critical in providing the advantage to the fish.

UNDERCUT BANKS. These sites offer numerous advantages including protection, shelter from the current, and yet easily accessible floating prey. The riparian vegetation of trees and shrubs may also provide an additional food source in the form of falling terrestrial insects as well as shade and shelter from avian predators.

RIFFLE-POOL JUNCTION. The turbulent water of the riffle environment often scours out a depression in the substrate of the pool. This deeper water affords protection yet permits easy access to the insects that dwell in the riffles.

TAILS OF POOLS. The depth and shape of the pool is the determining factor related to favorable trout habitat. As the current encounters the end of the pool, it generally speeds up because the tail of the pool is shallower and narrower than the middle. Obviously, if the current is too fast, trout may abandon this location. However, the narrower stream channel does offer the advantage of funneling the drifting food to the trout.

To a casual observer streams tend to be in a state of flux—changing their courses, undercutting their banks, and forming riffle-pool structures. The transport of water and sediment are the main physical agents that account for the long-term evolution of a stream channel. Over a period of time, if the amount of water and sediment that enters a particular stream reach is balanced by the amount leaving the reach, the stream has attained a state of dynamic equilibrium. This period of dynamic equilibrium may be short-lived if conditions in the stream's drainage basin change as a result of natural or anthropogenic activities. If torrential rains in the basin cause significant runoff and sediment input to the stream, the stream's velocity, depth, and cross-sectional area will change to restore its equilibrium state. These changes in the stream's physical characteristics may result in the stream creating a deeper channel, eroding its stream banks, or depositing large sediment loads in the form of bars or islands.

The sediment that is carried in the stream flow occurs in three forms: dissolved, suspended, and bed loads. The movement of water may result in rock and mineral ions being dissolved from the stream substrate. These dissolved ions, such as sodium, calcium, and potassium, are called the *dissolved load.* This component is not a significant factor in altering the shape and nature of the stream channel but can contribute to the saltiness of some lakes. Sediments range in size from clay-sized particles to gravel. After a rainstorm, creeks and streams may have a cloudy, brownish appearance as a result of suspended sediment washed in from the surrounding land. While the large sediment particle may settle out to the river bottom, the smaller clay and silt particles remain suspended in the water column as *suspended load.* Even slow-flowing currents can keep these small particles suspended. As will be seen in a later section, sediment-clogged rivers can have a detrimental effect on trout and salmon survivability. During extreme rainfall events and the resulting flooding, the increased stream flow is at a peak. During this period of maximum discharge, the current can move cobbles and boulders along the bottom as *bed load*. Though this component is relatively small compared to the suspended load, it results in the greatest morphological changes in the streambed.

Researchers recognize three states of stream channels that are out of equilibrium: incised channels, aggrading stream channels, and laterally unstable channels. One of the most frequent stream ailments, particularly in arid and semiarid climates, is the incised channel. This down-cut channel results when the erosive forces of high flows exceeds the capability of the streambed to resist erosion. The increased stream velocity may be the result of increased runoff from storms or land use changes, stream channelization, or degradation of buffering riparian vegetation. Once incision has been initiated, because the stream channel has been cut below the floodplain, the problem is that the channel-forming flood flows become restricted within the channel. This confined flow can be extremely erosive and continue to dramatically change the morphology of the stream.

An aggrading stream channel is one that is rising relative to the surrounding floodplain because its pools, depressions, and riffles are being filled with sediment. Essentially, the stream has lost its ability to transport its sediment load as a result of decreasing discharge. A laterally unstable channel is one characterized by a channel that is both increasing in width and decreasing in depth simultaneously. These channels occur when the natural streamside vegetation is severely altered or denuded, generally as a result of human activities. Without the soil-binding properties provided by the roots of the vegetation, the stream banks are susceptible to erosion during flood periods. The result is a wide and shallow stream that may harbor few suitable trout habitats.

SIX

Survival in a Fluid Environment

AS WE DISCOVERED IN THE PREVIOUS CHAPTER, the movement of water is critical to the well-being of stream-dwelling organisms. This concept of movement or flow is one of the main characteristics of a fluid. While air moves in the form of wind and water as a current, a solid does not flow. Hence, a fluid is either a gas or a liquid but definitely not a solid. A life immersed in a fluid—such as a flowing stream—is, of course, nothing out of the ordinary for an organism. The relationship of an organism to its fluid is complex; as current may flow across a sedentary critter, the organism moves against the current, and fluid passes through internal conduits. Obviously, to survive, organisms must contend with fluid motion. Part of this adaptation is in the design and morphology of the organism—to which much of this chapter will be devoted. Its intended message is that adaptations are of considerable interest, and the study of fluids need not be viewed with undue alarm or anxiety. While college courses in fluid mechanics can be quite intimidating, involving mastery of vector calculus and differential equations, we will resort to some simple physical models and relationships, a world in which the fly angler can feel quite at ease—or at least not wound too tightly.

Two important properties of water that distinguish it from other fluids are density and viscosity. *Density* is defined as the mass of an object divided by its volume. While a pound of feathers and iron will both have the same mass, the physical space (volume) occupied by the feathers will be considerably larger than for the iron—hence, its density is less. Fly lines float because they are impregnated with tiny air bubbles in the line surface, making their density less than that of water. The silk fly lines of our fly-fishing ancestors had to be oiled (dressing the line) in order to float, while horsehair lines floated so well that they were literally hard to sink.

Water, with a density of approximately 0.5 ounces per cubic inch, is approximately a thousand times denser than air. Because of the greater density of water compared to air, sound travels faster (four times faster) and farther in water than air; and this fact has an interesting application to a common fly-fishing situation. An angler who carelessly slaps a fly line on the water surface during the casting stroke should not be surprised to see every wary trout flee for cover. Stream-dwelling trout are easily spooked by any unnatural noises, such as clumsily wading through the water. Sound is transmitted as a vibration in the form of pressure waves that travel through water. These pressure waves span the spectrum from very high frequencies, ultrasound, to low frequencies that are detected as vibrations from the surroundings. Fish do not have external ears, but these sound vibrations are readily transmitted from the water though the fish's body to its internal ears. Though the trout's stream is naturally a noisy environment, any unusual vibrations are interpreted as warning signs.

Another direct effect of water's higher density is that it is a very supportive medium for the organisms immersed in it. This fact eliminates the need for the strong skeletal structure common in terrestrial organisms. A large fish that is allowed to stay out of the water for a protracted length of time may experience internal organ damage, since it is no longer has the support of its weight-bearing environment. As conscientious fly anglers, we should take care in handling a fish once it is out of the water. Most knowledgeable anglers will keep the fish at least partly immersed in the water and use a well-placed hand for additional support.

Though all fluids flow, the ease at which a fluid flows is called *viscosity*. We intuitively recognize differences in viscosity when we consider how honey pours (flows) from a jar compared to pouring water. Another view is to consider viscosity as a measure of the molecular "stickiness" between layers of fluid. Essentially water is a viscous medium that poses unique problems to its inhabitants. One problem that we will address is the viscosity-temperature relationship. Viscosity increases as temperature decreases. At 40°F water is about twice as viscous as at 95°F. While, as we will discuss in later chapters, trout are not tolerant of either these high or low temperatures, they do experience changes in temperatures on both a daily and seasonal basis. In this regard, researchers have raised a number of interesting questions: Does the variation of viscosity as a function of temperature have any biological implications? Does the blood of some animals behave like "multiviscosity" oils, minimizing the tendencies to thicken with decreasing temperature and to thin with increasing temperatures? This might be advantageous if the organism has to function with the same circulatory mechanisms at different temperatures. With regard to the latter question, research has shown that the viscosity of the blood of rainbow trout has unusually low temperature dependence.

Another role of viscosity is to inhibit movement of an organism through the fluid. While a world-class sprinter may be able to run 100 yards in under 10 seconds, a comparable athlete cannot swim the same distance in that time. But we're jumping ahead of ourselves and need to introduce additional physical principles pertaining to fluid flow.

One of the simplest models to visualize the movement of a fluid is a series of streamlines. While streamlines have a very specific meaning in fluid mechanics, we will simply refer to them as lines of current flow. Recall from the previous chapter the discussion of the role of in-stream rocks with regard to

FIG. 20. Water flow, visualized as a series of streamlines, around an obstacle

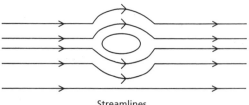

Streamlines

holding trout. The movement of the current as it encounters this obstacle can be viewed in figure 20 as a series of parallel streamlines that do not cross each other. Note the streamlines spread apart in front of the rock and recall that this location may hold trout due to decreased current speed. This issue can be elucidated by introducing the principle of continuity—the amount going in must equal the amount coming out. For example, if a specific volume of a fluid enters through one end of a pipe, the same volume must leave at the other end. In other words, the product of the fluid's velocity and the cross-sectional area of the pipe always remains the same as the fluid travels through the pipe (fig. 21). If the cross-sectional area of the pipe decreases to half of its initial size, its speed must double. Referring again to figure 20, note the spreading-apart (increasing area) of the streamlines in front of the obstacle. By the principle of continuity the speed of the current must decrease. We will shortly be seeing other applications of streamlines and the principle of continuity, but we need to introduce a few other properties and principles that apply to fluids.

FIG. 21. Flow through a pipe and the principle of continuity

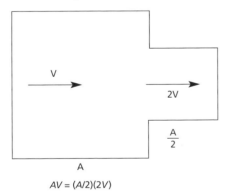

$$AV = (A/2)(2V)$$

In the chapter on the mechanical properties of rods we introduced the concept of force. While appropriate for solids, the concept of pressure is more applicable for fluids. *Pressure* is defined as a force divided by area over which the force is applied. For the same force applied by an object, the pressure will be greater if the object has a small surface area. For example, a sharp-pointed (small area) knife will penetrate farther into wood than a blunt-ended knife—the force being the same in both cases. An extension of this argument is one called hydrostatic pressure—a column of fluid of a specific height will exert a specific pressure on its bottom. The pressure is a function of only three variables—density, gravity, and height. When a fish dives below the water surface, the organism experiences an increase in hydrostatic pressure mainly as a result of increased depth. For example, a fish holding at a depth of 100 feet would experience a pressure of approximately 45 pounds on each square inch of its surface, compared to only 15 pounds per square inch for a fish at 33 feet. But since the pressure is exerted equally in all directions, even upward, the fish isn't accelerated in any particular direction as a consequence of that pressure.

But what about pressure caused by a moving (nonstatic) fluid, the type that cause trees to sway in the wind or that fish encounter in a swift current? Much of what we know in this area is based upon the work of Daniel Bernoulli, an eighteenth-century mathematician. His formulation, based upon a number of assumptions about the nature of a fluid, states that the sum of a pressure term, height term, and velocity term remains constant as a fluid flows through a pipe—Bernoulli's principle. For example, if the height (depth) of a fluid did not vary, the speed of the fluid would increase with a decrease in pressure and vice versa. The classic application of Bernoulli's principle is in regard to air flight. The lower surface of the plane's wing is flat, whereas the upper surface is curved. As air moves over the wing, it moves more rapidly over the top portion (bunching of streamlines) than over the lower surface. But this produces a pressure difference from bottom (higher pressure) to top (lower pressure) of the wing, resulting in lift. This discussion is all fine and dandy for its own intrinsic value, but let's get back to the stream.

As we wade into the stream to get closer to that trout, we are keenly aware of the current flow against our legs. If we are not careful, this current can cause us to lose our balance, because we feel the "drag" the current is exerting against our legs. If we consider a leg as a cylinder in the current flow, then the streamline flow would be similar to that in figure 20. Based upon Bernoulli's principle, the pressure should be relatively high and equal in the front and back of the cylinder and low and equal on the sides. Not only do the pressures cancel each other from front to back, but also along the sides. As a result there is no net pressure to carry the cylinder (leg) with the current—there is no "drag." But how can this be true? Have we imagined the incessant tugging of the water against our leg? Of course not, it's simply that theory doesn't always mesh with reality. Experiments have shown that, while pressure is relatively high in front of the object—theory and reality in agreement—rear pressure is low, resulting in a net pressure difference that we feel as "drag." One of the main reasons that theory and experiment do not agree is that Bernoulli considered an "ideal" fluid, not in the sense that it is perfect in nature, but that it does not incorporate all properties of a fluid—namely viscosity. But recall viscosity is one of the defining characteristics of a fluid. In order to address this issue we have to distinguish between two types of flow. *Laminar flow* can be viewed as a smooth, sheetlike movement of water layers with little vertical mixing between the layers—essentially parallel streamlines. By contrast, irregular movement within the fluid and considerable mixing between layers characterize *turbulent flow.* An example of turbulent flow is the "bumpiness" sometimes experienced in air travel.

The famous hydrodynamicist Osborne Reynolds (1842–1912) was first to define the nature of turbulence in 1883 by performing some empirical experiments with water flowing through a pipe. He discovered that the flow became turbulent if the velocity, pipe diameter, or fluid density increased beyond a certain point. His work led to a new player in the field of biological fluid mechanics—the Reynolds number. This number is simply the product of the velocity, size, and density divided by dynamic viscosity. With regard to water flowing in a stream, we can for all practical purposes consider the density and viscosity as relatively constant for a particular time and look at the current velocity and size of the stream. If either one of these variables increases, there is a transition from laminar to turbulent flow. In the stream, the flow behind the obstacle is very turbulent, and the pressure decreases downstream. The final upshot is high pressure upstream of the obstacle and low pressure downstream—the pressure difference that the fly-fisher experiences on her leg.

Now let's move our discussion to one of the more interesting primary effects of water movement on an organism—its ability to move through the fluid. Predator fish must be proficient at propelling their body through the water in order to capture prey. Prey fish must exhibit the same degree of mobility if they are to avoid capture. In nature, some organisms are the Corvettes of the aquatic environment, and others are the big, lumbering sedans that provide security if not speed.

In order for a fish to achieve maximum efficiency in the fundamental process of locomotion, it must overcome the viscous nature of water that results in a frictional drag. While I previously used this term to describe that tugging sensation on the legs due to the current flow, I'll be a little more rigorous in its definition and application. *Drag* is a force that impedes movement through a fluid and can be portioned into two components. *Surface drag* is the friction between the surface of the body and the surrounding water. The more surface area exposed to the fluid, the greater the surface drag. In the swimming venues during the 2000 summer Olympics in Sydney, Australia, some of those world-class swimmers donned specialized suits that claimed to minimize this component of drag. Fish have their own natural covering, a mucous secretion or slime that has been shown in some cases to reduce the skin friction significantly. It also appears that slimes from faster fish tend to be the most effective. The effect of surface drag decreases with increasing turbulence, and pressure drag tends to dominate at a higher Reynolds number. *Pressure drag* is a function of the volume of water that must be pushed aside by a moving body. It results from the pressure gradient that exists between the upstream side of an object and its downstream side. Pressure drag increases proportionally to the cross-sectional area of the body. For example, a flat object oriented perpendicular to the current would experience significant drag. Empirical studies have shown that this drag is minimized when elongated objects are oriented parallel to the current and have a tapering posterior section—streamlined. Researchers can construct objects in the laboratory that are highly streamlined, but what do we see in nature with regard to form and shape? What about our trout trying to survive in a strong current?

To answer these questions, the reader must first be acquainted with various body shapes of aquatic organisms. Biologists have identified four distinct shapes: compressed, depressed, attenuated, and fusiform. Fish exhibiting a *compressed* body shape are narrow in width, as opposed to *depressed* body shapes, which are flattened when viewed from above or below. Organisms with an *attenuated* shape are elongated, or eel-like. A *fusiform* shape tapers at both ends with a relatively thicker midsection. Of these four shapes, the latter is the most streamlined. As a fusiform-shaped fish moves through the water, the flow of water over the organism is relatively smooth and uniform, streamlines are intact, and wake is reduced (fig. 22). In contrast, a compressed-shaped fish is poorly streamlined, creating a significant wake (fig. 22). A significant pressure

FIG. 22. Flow over and behind a streamlined and nonstreamlined fish

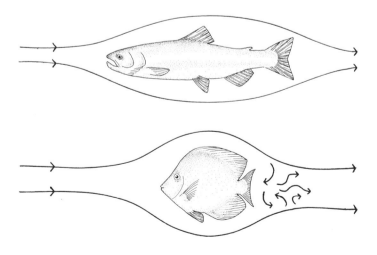

gradient is created from front to rear of the fish—resulting in drag. In effect, since pressure is a force, the fish is essentially being pushed back as it swims. Salmon and trout (fig. 23), while not exhibiting the classic fusiform shape found in members of the tuna family that can reach speeds of over 50 miles per hour, exhibit a modified fusiform shape that makes them highly suited to moving through water. Studies have shown that, in order to minimize drag, the width-to-length ratio of fish should equal one-fourth. For example, a 24-inch-long trout should have a width of no more than 6 inches to achieve maximum efficiency. While many modern designers of drag-minimizing vehicles have looked to nature for inspiration, Sir George Cayley (1773–1857) was a pioneer in this area. He proposed that the shape of the rear portion of the object in question was just as important as the front section in decreasing resistance. When his proposal was not widely accepted in the scientific community, he selected a biological model, the trout, which he guessed was a low-drag organism. He took girth measurements along the length of the trout from which he constructed a simple profile of the trout. It wasn't till almost a hundred years after his death that it was recognized that his profile corresponds almost exactly to that of a modern low-drag airplane wing.

FIG. 23. Example of a salmonid

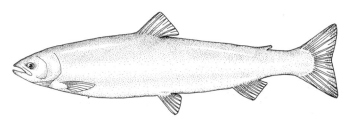

A more detailed view of the anatomy of a fish is necessary to understand other aspects of locomotion such as turning, maneuverability, and acceleration. What anatomically distinguishes fish from other aquatic organisms is their fins. In conjunction with the fish's musculature these fins play a critical role in the fish's adapting to its fluid environment. The pectoral fins are paired fins located behind the gill cover. A trout, holding in a current, tilts its pectoral fins to rise slowly to the surface to sip prey and then reorients these fins to slowly descend to its station. The dorsal fin(s) and anal fin, located on the top and bottom of the fish respectively, play a key role in maintaining a stable orientation of the fish in a stream. (In addition, the upper portion of a fish's ear provides a sense of balance in its turbulent environment. The three fluid-filled semicircular canals in this part of the ear are arranged so that one gives yaw, another pitch, and the last roll.)

In a buffering current the fish must be able to remain upright to extract oxygen from the water and to locate and feed upon prey. The pelvic fins, on the underside of the fish, are utilized in other aspects of maneuvering such as turning and braking. Propulsion in a fish is a complex interaction between body movements and the tail, or caudal fin. The basic movement of a swimming trout is an undulating motion extending from the head to the tail. These undulations are slight in the anterior portion of the fish but increase significantly toward the rear. In principle, no part of the body travels in a straight line. Even the snout of the fish oscillates at small amplitudes about the mean path of the fish (Hoar and Randall 1978). These undulations are achieved by the alternate contraction and expansion of muscle segments along the sides of the body. The alternating sweep of the caudal fin, "fishtailing," exerts a back-pressure that provides the forward thrust of the fish.

Frequency of tail beats and the rate at which the waves travel along the body determine the speed. These two factors are directly related to the musculature of the fish in question. Most fish have a combination of both white and red muscle tissue. On the average, about 20 percent of a trout's muscle tissue is red; most is white. What is the significance of white versus red muscle tissue? Red muscle fibers contain higher concentrations of myoglobin, a red pigment with an affinity for oxygen. Red muscle tissues, therefore, obtain a much greater oxygen supply than white muscles. They support a metabolic rate six times higher than that of white muscles, needed for endurance and prolonged swimming. Stream-dwelling trout need very little red tissue, since they are not continually swimming but holding in the current and waiting for prey to be swept by. The white muscle tissues, which fatigue quite quickly, are adequate for short bursts of speed to capture the prey.

In addition, the speed of the fish depends partially upon the shape of the caudal fin. A useful function for assessing the swimming style of a fish is the *aspect ratio:*

$$AR = \text{height of caudal fin}^2/\text{area of caudal fin}$$

Consider a caudal fin with a height and width of 4 inches. The surface area of the fin is 16 (4 in by 4 in) square inches. This is divided into the height squared (16 sq in) for an aspect ratio of 1. If we modify the caudal fin to have the same height but a width of only 2 inches, the aspect ratio is 4. Increasing aspect ratios are positively correlated with increasing fish speed. Why is this so? A caudal fin that is broad, having a large surface area, can develop significant push against the water for rapid acceleration or maneuverability. But the downside is that the large surface area increases drag, resulting in loss of forward speed. In contrast, fast-cruising fish have caudal fins with minimum surface area but maximum spread between the dorsal and ventral lobes of the fin. These fish are slow to obtain maximum speed, since they cannot develop the initial thrust, but can maintain high speeds due to decreased frictional drag once they get going.

There are four shapes of caudal fins that have been identified with regard to propulsion in fish. The rounded fin (fig. 24) is a relatively flexible fin that lends itself to brief bursts of acceleration and maneuverability at slow speeds ($AR = 1$). This tail shape is characteristic of prey fish that must seek shelter to avoid predation by swifter fish. The truncate fin (fig. 24), characteristic of trout and salmon, offers increased maneuverability and acceleration ($AR = 3$). Stream-dwelling trout are engaged in a number of activities—holding within the current, seeking shelter when threatened, and foraging for prey. The relatively broad area of the truncate fin provides sufficient push to counter the force of the current, providing it is not too strong. You can often see trout calmly "waving" their tail as they maintain their position in the current. Food items tumbling along with the current are still readily accessible to the trout, since the somewhat flexible tail allows for ease in change of direction. A nervous trout can rapidly accelerate from its feeding station to an undercut bank or protective log as a clumsy angler spooks it. It can't maintain this speed for any duration, but it doesn't need to, since shelter may only be a fly cast away. A study (Webb 1991) of the swimming style of rainbow trout showed that the motion is never constant but involves acceleration, deceleration, and turning.

FIG. 24 Caudal tail shapes: rounded; truncate; forked; lunate

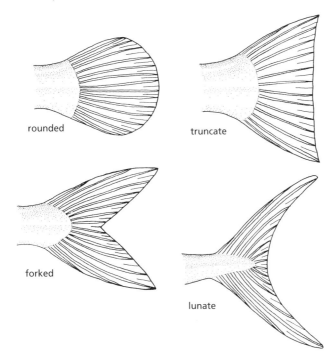

Adult salmon returning to spawn in the headwaters of their natal rivers encounter formidable obstacles in the upstream journey. They not only must overcome the constant flow of the current but also navigate numerous cataracts. The

broad sweep of the tail and the resultant thrust it generates allows the salmon to leap the numerous waterfalls and steep rapids it may encounter on its upstream migration.

The forked fin (fig. 24) is generally characteristic of fish that must actively hunt for food ($AR = 5$). While stream-dwelling fish have the luxury of the current to convey their food, certain lake, estuarine, and ocean fish must search their relatively stagnant environment to locate and capture prey. At the apex are the fast cruisers (sustained rapid swimming) such as tuna, having a lunate fin (fig. 24). The fin is very rigid and relatively useless in maneuverability but very efficient in attaining and maintaining top-end speeds ($AR = 8$). Biologists have shown a good correlation between the type of swimming and success in capturing prey. Fish with lunate fins cover large stretches of the watery realm but, because of their limited turning ability, do not capture a significant number of fish from the pods of bait fish they encounter.

As we have previously discussed, trout employ several strategies to minimize the energy-sapping effect of the current. Another energy-conserving tactic utilized by numerous organisms living in a fluid is gliding. This smooth, effortless motion is probably best exemplified in the soaring of birds on air currents. Albatrosses, which have been known to stay aloft for an extended period of time, are probably the masters of this aerodynamic art. But it also seems probable that gliding, albeit to a limited extent, is in the repertoire of aquatic organisms. When we think of the "top-gun gliders" in the avian community, the first characteristic that may come to mind is the long wingspan of these birds. While this is certainly very important, it is not the total story. We have to return to the Reynolds number.

While it is an indicator of the turbulence of a fluid, another view is that this number is a measure of the relative importance of the inertial forces (the product of the density, size, and speed) to viscous effects. Though we are now familiar with the nature of viscosity, inertial forces relate to the tendency of an object to keep moving. Your fly line continues its forward movement even after you have stopped your casting stroke because of its inertia. A high Reynolds number means that the inertial forces tend to dominate over viscous effects. Objects set in motion will continue to keep moving in the fluid. This statement reflects the fact that inertial forces are proportional to the size and speed of the object under consideration. Simply put, big, fast objects have a greater inertia than small, slow objects. For example, a supertanker may require several miles to come to a complete stop even though it is no longer under power. Its massive size and speed have generated considerable inertia. In contrast, a tiny organism moving at very low speed will stop almost immediately because of the sticky, viscous nature of the fluid. From table 3 compare the Reynolds number for a spectrum of swimming organisms of various sizes and speeds. Research has shown that when the Reynolds number is above 1,000 inertial forces dominate. While trout do not have the size or speed of a tuna, they can generate considerable inertia—meaning they can glide a distance through their viscous environment. So they achieve energy economy by alternately accelerating and gliding. Our leaping salmon also depends upon its considerable inertia to overcome the in-stream obstacles.

Now, we have seen that the trout and salmon are marvelously structured both in form and size to survive and prosper within their fluid environment. To further expand our knowledge, let us view the morphology of the trout as a function of its low drag profile. As water flows over our streamlined trout, the velocity decreases (principle of continuity) and the pressure increases (Bernoulli principle) on its head; that is,

TABLE 3. Swimming organisms and their Reynolds numbers

Organism	Reynolds number
Large whale swimming at 30 ft/s	300,000,000
Tuna swimming at 30 ft/s	30,000,000
Copepod swimming at 10 in/s	30,000
Bacterium swimming at 0.0004 in/s	0.00001

Source: Data chiefly from Vogel (1994)

the pressure is directed inward. Farther back, the pressure is directed outward. In the region where the fish experiences inward pressure, it has a compression-resistant skull. Behind the head, where the pressure is directed outward, a flexible, stretchable skin is adequate to maintain normal shape. It has been proposed that this pressure difference from the anterior to the posterior regions of the body facilitates oxygen transfer through the gills—to take in water where pressure is directed inward and eject water where pressure is directed outward.

Our discussions thus far have examined the effect of a moving fluid on an object or the movement of fish relative to the fluid. Let me now present a different approach and view the transfer of fluids from within the organism to the environment and vice versa. I'm sure most of us are familiar with the expression "drinking like a fish." Is there any truth to this statement, and, if there is, do we mean a saltwater fish or freshwater fish? I'll now try to answer these questions so that at least you can use this material to impress your guests at your next party.

Freshwater fish and marine fish live in distinctively different environments partly as a result of differences in the amount of dissolved ions in the water. This is commonly referred to as salinity, or simply the saltiness of the water. The average salinity of the freshwater and marine environments is o percent and 3.5 percent, respectively. When there are differences in salinity, the process of osmosis results in the movement of pure water across a membrane from a compartment with relatively low salinity to a compartment with high salinity. While this may be a nice formal definition, let's see its application to our fish. A biological process unique to many aquatic organisms is *osmoregulation*—the ability to regulate the concentration of dissolved ions in its body irrespective of changes in the environment. The salinity of the body fluids of a freshwater fish, like trout, is about 1.0 percent, compared to roughly o percent for the water. This difference makes the trout hypertonic relative to the fluid in which it resides. The trout's problem is to avoid diffusing into its body excessive quantities of water that will rupture its cell walls. To prevent this fluid imbalance the trout must excrete copious amounts of dilute urine into the environment and not drink any water. In contrast, marine fish are *hypotonic:* that is, the salinity of their body fluids (0.8–1.4%) is less than that of seawater (3.5%). In this case, marine fish would dehydrate due to loss of water from their bodies into the environment. Marine fish drinking saltwater and excreting the salts through their gills counteract the loss. To further conserve fluids, marine fish excrete only small amounts of urine to the environment. Salmon are unique with regard to osmoregulation as compared to strictly freshwater or marine fish. Salmon are *anadromous*—spawn in fresh water and then migrate to the ocean to grow to maturity. The physiological changes are quite complex, and salmon must have an appropriate period for this adjustment. In particular, ocean salmon that are returning to spawn in their natal rivers may at first be reluctant to take a fly, since they are literally "out of balance" with their fluid environment.

We have now seen how fish can move through their fluid environment to capture prey or patiently wait for the flow to bring them their food item. The next chapter deals with the nature and type of prey found on the menu of trout.

SEVEN

What Fish Eat: The Diet of Trout

WITH MY FIRST PURCHASED FLY ROD IN HAND, I set out to a local stream to hone my fly casting skills. It wasn't long before I was in the rhythm of the casting stroke, feeling content that I had made the right decision to begin pursuing the art of fly-fishing. My tranquil moment was abruptly interrupted by a swarm of insects that emerged from out of nowhere. As these insects settled upon the water surface, swirls of water could be seen dimpling the surface. As a neophyte fly angler, I made no connection between these two activities and was simply annoyed that none other than some bugs were rudely interrupting my casting practice. It wasn't until that evening in a conversation with a more experienced angler that I learned I had witnessed a fundamental ritual of trout—fish rising to feed voraciously on aquatic insects. Appropriately humbled, I realized I needed to learn more about the arcane world of insect behavior. The study of insects is fascinating in itself and requires no angling justification, but such knowledge will pay off handsomely when on the water.

In his seminal article entitled "The Practical Entomologist," Carl Richards posed the following questions to the reader: Should an angler study entomology? Is it that important to angling success? His response to the latter inquiry was a resounding yes. The angler who wants to catch more and larger fish is strongly encouraged by Richards to pursue the discipline of entomology. This entomological wave of creativity continued with the publication of Ernest Schwiebert's *Matching the Hatch* (1955), which emphasized the trout's selectivity in its dietary habits and how anglers can counteract this apparent advantage. His argument is that trout can be highly discriminating in choosing their food, and the angler who does not recognize the type of insect chosen by the trout will often be defeated in his effort to catch fish. Though the angler may possess the ability to identify fish holding places and delicately present a fly to a trout that is not yet aware of his presence, these skills may be of little value if the trout spurns the offered fly from the caster. Being able to identify and match the insects on which trout feed can mean the difference between catching fish or telling fish tales. And yet this skill is often the one missing in the angler's repertoire.

So, to be a successful fly angler, it is important to know what the trout eats, and why, and when. But don't despair! It is not necessary to do graduate work in entomology, perform detailed microscopic analysis of insect larvae, or memorize a myriad of Latin names. Even keeping it relatively simple, you can still fool a number of fish in a favorite stream. Let's go over our game plan for understanding the trout-insect relationship.

First, what do trout eat? Studies have shown that the diet of a trout in a stream is heavily dependent upon aquatic insects. This group comprises approximately 90 percent of the food items consumed by trout. Obviously, the beginning fly angler needs to concentrate on these organisms but not to the exclusion of the remaining 10 percent—terrestrial insects (6%), minnows (3%), and crustaceans (1%). The key to any successful fly-angling adventure is observation. Before you start flailing the water with your fly rod, take the time to watch what aquatic insects the trout are consuming. You can keep it simple at this stage. Did that rising trout take the big cream-colored fly or the small gray one? You'll have to focus and concentrate at this stage in order to distinguish between surface and subsurface feeding.

Before going to the stream, you should be familiar with the appearance of the dominant insects in your area. This is not as daunting as it may first seem, since the number of major insects at any particular time is relatively small. A key point to remember is that stream insects hatch in batches during a particular time of the year. While seasonal temperature fluctuation

TABLE 4. Seasonal hatches in the eastern United States

Months	Type of Insect
March to May	Dark-colored insects
May to June	Yellow- to tan-colored insects
July to August	Big insects
September to October	Tiny insects

may retard or advance this activity to a certain extent, you can depend upon the consistency of a yearly progression of hatches in your region. Table 4 provides you with a guideline for seasonal hatches within the eastern United States.

Admittedly, this information is quite general. There will be situations that require a greater in-depth understanding of insect types. For example, I know that in my area at the beginning of April there are only two significant hatches that I need to focus on: quill gordons and black caddis. But how do you obtain that information? The local fly shop can be a good starting point, since they are obviously in the business of selling flies that imitate insects that catch fish. A knowledgeable owner can be an indispensable resource to help match the hatch. Members of the local chapter of Trout Unlimited, a conservation organization dedicated to a healthy trout population in the United States, are also willing to aid in assessing the major insects within the streams. There is simply no substitute for local information, and there is no fun in ignorance and inefficiency.

Fish smarter, not harder. Imagine yourself on a remote, pristine mountain stream with trout rising all around and flies buzzing in the air and drifting on the current. How do you, under the pressure to catch these fish, select the correct fly to imitate these naturals? That's the crux of this discussion, isn't it? If we choose correctly, our chances of success increase dramatically; otherwise we face the proverbial skunking. Our first task is to catch some of these insects (not the fish yet) and determine what these insects are. You'll have to do this only once or twice until you're familiar with the dominant insects of that stream. Catching these flies is relatively simple. An aquarium net can scoop up flies floating on the surface, and those airborne can be gathered with a butterfly net. If there are no insects visible, a seine test will quickly yield information on subsurface aquatic forms. The seine is held in the current while some gentle kicking disturbs the bottom. Whatever is dislodged is washed into the seine. If this activity seems to be rather pedestrian to you, then by all means involve your family. What kid doesn't like to catch some bugs? Upon collection, it is not necessary to know their names but only to determine which of the flies in your collection best imitate these insects. Examination of the insects is best accomplished on the stream bank with the aid of a small magnifying glass. There are three characteristics of any insect you should keep in mind when attempting a match: size, shape, and color. Select an appropriate artificial from your fly box, and you should be ready to pursue your quarry. Note that this whole process follows a sequence of logical steps: patient collection, careful examination, and selection of imitation.

The above information is a starting point and will allow you to be a competent angler. But this chapter was also written with the curious angler in mind, the angler who is not completely satisfied with the "cookbook" approach to matching insects but wants to know more about this fascinating trout-insect relationship. Let's begin our journey!

By now we are familiar with the fact that the aquatic insect group deserves our attention. The four major aquatic insect orders that emerge from our streams are mayflies *(Ephemeroptera)*, caddisflies *(Tichoptera)*, stoneflies *(Plecoptera)*, and midges *(Diptera)*. Being an effective hatch-matcher requires the ability to quickly differentiate between the adult stage of the mayflies, caddisflies, midges, and stoneflies and the immature stage of these orders.

MAYFLIES. There are about five hundred species of mayflies in North America, with their origin dating back over 300 million years as recorded in the fossil record. When one thinks of fly casting for trout, the mayfly holds a lofty position, having been praised and written about for over five hundred years. The earliest written reference to the mayfly was by Dame Juliana Berners in 1496 describing the dressings of flies that closely resemble the form of a mayfly. Such eminent writers as Izaak Walton and Charles Cotton maintained its place in fly-fishing lore during the 1600s. Cotton, in particular, describes in detail sixty-five trout flies that imitate the mayfly. Currently, its esteemed position in the eyes of fly anglers is well deserved, since mayflies are generally the most important food item of a trout's diet.

Their upright wings, which have been colorfully described as boat sails, identify one of the most striking examples in the insect world, adult mayflies (fig. 25). Within the mayfly family, different species can be identified primarily by their varying wing color and translucency. Coloration ranges from light creams and yellows to dark grays and browns. Prominent tails (two to three) and an upward-curved body round out the distinguishing characteristics of this insect. Their delicate physical appearance and graceful flight make mayflies the gossamers of the insect world.

FIG. 25. Mayfly

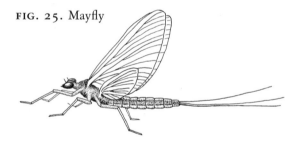

The life cycle of the mayfly consists of four distinct stages: egg, nymph, dun, and spinner. An adult mayfly lays its eggs on the surface of the water, most often in riffles, and frequently in the evening. The knowledgeable angler will fish the riffles during the twilight period as hungry trout move in to make a meal of the spawning mayflies. Soon after sinking into the crevices of the stream bottom, the eggs hatch into tiny larvae, or nymphs, ranging in size from 0.2 inches to 1.4 inches. This stage can be the most productive one for the fly angler in light of the fact that most studies have shown that trout acquire the major portion of their food below the water surface, and nymphs are generally available year-round in a stream. Taking their cues from the physical environment, nymphs have evolved in appearance to meet the rigors of the stream environment. They are generally drab in color, allowing them to blend in with the stream bottom. The predominant colors are brown, green, and tan.

Before proceeding to the next life stage, let us pause to touch on the basic nymph types: crawlers, swimmers, burrowers, and clingers. Each is equipped with specific physical and morphological characteristics enabling it to adapt to its unique habitat. For example, the species that cling to the bottom have streamlined bodies—a blunt front and tapered rear—that allows them to counter the turbulent drag induced by the current flow. In a study conducted during the 1920s a comparison was made of nymphs that occupied fast-flowing streams to those from less-turbulent waters. Individuals preferring rapid flows are generally smaller and have larger legs. But what was particularly interesting is the cross-sectional shape of the legs. The femurs and tibias are flattened, thicker at the anterior portions and thinner at the posterior margins— that is, streamlined. From the prospective of the fly angler, imitations should take into account these dominant body shapes and the limited range in coloration. So even though there are hundreds of nymph species, a general representation of the shape, color, and size of the nymph will allow the taking of fish in most cases.

Almost exactly one year after they hatch from eggs, the nymphs embark on their next developmental stage. Stimulated by physical factors such as water temperature and sunlight, nymphs migrate to the surface by gases released from inside their exoskeleton. When the nymph reaches the surface, it sheds its exoskeleton; and a winged form, called a dun, emerges onto the water surface. The term *dun* arises from the dun (gray) color of the emerging mayfly's wings. Some species of nymphs may emerge at the same time of day for a few days, while others may emerge sporadically throughout the day for almost a month. Fly anglers commonly refer to the emergence of the dun as "the hatch."

During its preoccupation with emergence, the dun is very vulnerable to predation. The newly emerged dun must rest on the water surface to dry its wings before it flies off to a streamside bush or tree. Floating on the water, they are subject to the relentless attack of the hungry trout. You should note that, during this period, trout become very selective with regard to physical size, shape, and color. These hatches may not last very long, so your ability to analytically and calmly determine the appropriate fly pattern can spell the difference between hooking your share of fish or muttering to yourself.

Those duns that survive the onslaught of the marauding trout slowly rise from the surface, heading to the protective cover of the streamside vegetation to enter into their final life stage. After resting for a day or two to mature, the dun molts, its wings becoming window-clear, the body darkening, and the tails lengthening. The flies then form into mating swarms over stream riffles, swooping and swirling in the air, thus earning the name *spinner*. After mating, the females lay their eggs on the surface of the river and fall dead (spent) into the river. Having completed their life cycle, these spent spinners are gobbled up by greedy trout.

During the spinner fall, the correct imitation has both its wings and tails flat to the water surface. To take advantage of this opportunity, fish the evening or dusk periods, since these time frames generally coincide with maximum spinner falls. As compared to the splashier rise of trout to the duns, their movement toward the spent spinners is more deliberate and controlled. The trout seem to sense that these insects will not elude them, and they go about their feeding business in a leisurely fashion. For those readers who desire even more in-depth information regarding this unique aquatic insect, please refer to the exhaustive work *Hatches II* (1986) by Al Caucci and Bob Nastasi.

CADDISFLIES. Caddisflies often rival mayflies as an important food source for trout and therefore warrant attention.

As with all flies, the angler must be able to match the natural with an imitation. Simple observation is not sufficient, as proper identification involves collection and examination. This is often easier said than done, since these frenetic flies are quite jumpy and wary and often avoid the futile attempts of an amateur collector. Since caddisflies are naturally attracted to bright lights, the chances of capturing them in the evening can be increased by using an artificial light source, such as a flashlight or car lights, to lure them to a net.

Upon examination, adult caddisflies can be recognized by their inverted vee or tentlike wings that are folded parallel to their body (fig. 26). While relatively small in size, ¼ inch or less, the wings of the caddisfly may reach 150 percent of their body length—giving the impression of a much larger insect in flight. As contrasted to mayflies, caddisflies have long antennae but do not have the slender, delicate tails. With hundreds and perhaps thousands of this species, it is beyond the realm of the average angler to identify all of these insects. Don't feel disheartened, since few of the country's eminent entomologists can perform this task. A good approach is to carry some of the common patterns that imitate the major characteristics—shape, wing pattern, and coloration—of this insect.

In addition to appearance differences, the life cycle of the caddis differs markedly from that of mayfly. It includes the following four stages: egg, larva, pupa, and adult. The eggs are deposited in or near the water, eventually hatching into a larva. The great majority of caddis larvae build cases from pieces of gravel, twigs, and bits of vegetation. Each species has its own preference as to the type and size of debris it uses for its case, and species of caddis can be identified by the type and shape of the case. The case is utilized by the larvae for protection from predators and as an anchor against the flow of the current. Trout aren't always fooled by this camouflage, and examination of the stomach contents of a fish may reveal bits of sticks and gravel, which means it's a good bet that trout was feeding on caddis larvae or else had been making some errors in judgment. While I don't want to overly anthropomorphize the nature of trout, they do make mistakes that fortunately allow us to fool them. Other caddis larva are free-living, meaning they roam among the rocks on the bottom, unencumbered by a case. Living alongside mayfly nymphs, these larvae are readily available food items for the bottom-foraging trout.

As opposed to mayflies, caddisflies have a stage between the larva and the adult, known as the pupa. This occurs when the larva makes a cocoon in which it changes into a pupa. Upon maturation, the pupa cuts its way out of the cocoon and ascends to the surface. During this ascent, they are easy pickings for the trout. Those that survive this journey may drift a long distance within the water's surface film—again being subjected to the attack of the trout. During this drifting phase, a pupal imitation fished just below the surface can be quite deadly.

FIG. 26. Caddisfly

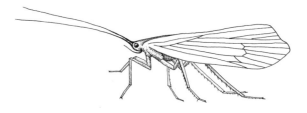

From the surviving pupae emerge the adult caddisflies—looking very much like tiny, drab moths. At this time caddisfly behavior differs markedly from that of the mayfly. Some species hop, skid, and flutter on the surface. Some ride the currents, providing an easy meal for trout and great sport for the fly angler who has correctly matched this hatch. A large number of these flies leave the water immediately, not even pausing to acclimate themselves to their new environment. Splashy rises signal frantic trout eagerly pursing their escaping prey.

The adult caddis has a longer life span than the mayfly. Living up to a month before they mate and die, they may feed actively during this period. During mating, they may often form huge swarms at dusk, skittering on the water to deposit their eggs and stimulating trout to feed on the surface. The rising trout sees only the body of the egg-laying adult and will key in on its color and size. While wing color and pattern are important to us in identifying the caddis, from the trout's underwater perspective they are not significant. Most fish will respond favorably to imitations that have the matching silhouette and size of the naturals.

STONEFLIES. While mayflies and caddisflies are found in all areas of a trout stream, from fast riffles to still pools, stoneflies are found in turbulent, highly oxygenated rocky streams. In some rivers, these relatively large insects comprise the major food source for trout. In fact, the famous salmonfly of western rivers is the largest trout stream insect, almost 3 inches long, and provides for some of the most spectacular fishing in the United States. The old saying—big flies catch big fish—may have some validity to it, as even the largest trout in these streams will feed on the salmonfly.

FIG. 27. Stonefly

The adult stage of this robust fly features hard, shiny, and markedly veined wings that fold flat over its back (fig. 27). Most stoneflies have noticeable antennae and two prominent short tails. For the beginning angler, the stonefly is the simplest to fish of all the flies. It is a food item for trout in only its nymph and egg-laying adult stages. The nymphs usually inhabit fast water and rapids, sharing this habitat with clinger mayfly nymphs. Their flattened shape makes them well suited for this turbulent environment. When mature, the nymphs crawl from the water to hatch on land. While trout will feed voraciously on a well-presented stonefly nymph imitation, the land hatchers are unavailable to the trout unless they fall or are blown into the water. The adults look exactly like the nymphs with the notable exception of their newly formed wings. Almost comical in flight, they resemble little helicopters, whirling around in the air. Upon maturation, stoneflies mate over water in dense swarms, fall spent to the water, and become irresistible food morsels for hungry trout. The egg-layers are well imitated by dark flies with a lot of hackle to mimic their moving wings.

MIDGES. As their name suggests, midges are quite tiny, resembling mosquitoes but with no beak to bite. Imitations of these gnat-sized organisms should be found within a well-stocked fly box, since these flies are especially important to trout in the slower currents of spring creeks and limestone streams. As opposed to stoneflies, they rarely inhabit the fast-moving waters of freestone streams. Since they hatch all year round, they provide a steady supply of food for the trout, particularly in the lean winter months when no other hatches are prevalent. But fishing midge hatches can try the patience and send a person scurrying to the optometrist for an eye exam. When trout are feeding on midges, they can be frustratingly picky in their selections. While they can and readily do discriminate between imitations tied on tiny hooks (approximately a quarter of an inch), the eye-strained angler is hard-pressed to see this speck on the water surface. All tackle, including rods, reels, leaders, and flies, is scaled down to make this fishing one of the ultimate challenges in fly-angling.

Midges exhibit a life cycle similar to that of caddisflies, with larval, pupal, and adult stages. Hatching in water, midges live the majority of their lives as larvae on the bottom of the stream. At this stage, they resemble tiny red, pink, or brown worms that burrow into the bottom of slow-moving streams. Like caddis, they turn to pupae before emerging as adults. All three stages are important to trout, the pupal stage being the most important, since the defenseless, drifting pupa are easy pickings for the trout. When midges are active, float a pupa imitation of the proper size and color in the water's surface film. In the vernacular of fly-fishing, angling that involves any tiny flies, such as minute mayflies (*Tricorythoses, Baetis*) falls under the heading *midge fishing,* though technically not so.

As pointed out previously, trout feed on other food items in addition to aquatic insects but to a much lesser extent. However, when summer hatches of mayflies, caddisflies, and stoneflies become rare, trout turn to terrestrial insects to meet their food needs—so a few representative imitations are to be included in the arsenal. A large trout's explosive rise to a fat grasshopper is an event that will cause even veteran anglers to have weak knees. So as you wander the fields of summer, stop to pick up the ever-present grasshopper. If upon placing this insect on the surface film there is a tremendous swirl of water and an acceptance of your offering, then you know to break out the terrestrials. Trout seem to relish ants, and, in the fall, large swarms of winged ants are quite prevalent. As with certain aquatic insects, trout again become very selective, and the angler must adjust accordingly by selecting the matching imitation with regard to body shape and color. Other terrestrial insects such as beetles, crickets, leafhoppers, and inchworms find their way into the stomach of trout. Terrestrial insects are important to trout where stream bank vegetation overhangs the water surface. Windy days result in these insects being blown into the water where hungry trout will be on the lookout for them. If all the flies discussed above weren't enough for the angler to imitate, other trout food items enter the picture: dragonflies and damselflies (nymph is the major stage in lakes and ponds), crustaceans (imitations of scuds, sowbugs, shrimp, and crayfish), and forage fish (darters, sculpins, and members of the minnow family). Exhausted yet? Remember fly-fishing knowledge is a lifelong pursuit.

An observant angler who has done some homework on the types and life stages of aquatic insects should by now be able to choose the appropriate pattern to match the hatch of a particular insect. Though not as common as the single hatch, on particularly productive streams, there are times that multiple hatches can occur, resulting in a bewildering array of insects from different species of mayflies to caddis and stoneflies. During this period, the trout can be maddeningly selective as a result of the large number of food items readily available. They may choose the dun and totally ignore the pupa—an ideal time for the trout but not for the frustrated angler.

How does one handle this situation? What imitations best address the selectivity of the trout? These are difficult questions to answer, and even seasoned anglers do not always agree on the correct approach to multiple hatches. One trap that the angler does not want to fall into is that of selecting fly patterns through trial and error in the hope of fooling a trout. This random, scattered approach will only lead to failure, since big old trout don't attain this status by being duped very often. On these occasions, there is no substitute for experience, knowledge, and keen observation. But I'll present a few pointers as offered by the dean of fly-fishing entomology, Carl Richards. First, in the presence of such vast food choices, the trout will feed on the most abundant insect. It is not unusual for trout to be feeding exclusively on small flies available in large numbers and to spurn the small number of large flies. A natural inclination of many anglers is to use the larger fly, but this should be avoided and be replaced by careful observation to determine which natural is most abundant.

Another tip is to try to identify the water pattern left by the rising trout. Trout will rise very stealthily and deliberately to insects that are small and cannot escape, such as mayfly spinners. Small, concentric rings will spread out from where the trout has dimpled the water surface. Splashy rises indicate fish taking insects that are fluttering on the surface, attempting to escape. A down-wing dry fly of the correct size and color should work. Then try to identify if the trout is actually feeding at the surface or just below it. Just before a hatch, subsurface feeding is quite common. Trout feeding just under the surface can be exasperating. You incorrectly interpret the fish's activity and toss a high-floating dry fly his way. Though he may lunge at it, he ultimately spurns the offering. Did he miss it? Not likely since an adult seldom misses its target. This should be a clue to put away the dry flies and fish a wet fly just under the surface, an emerger pattern, or a floating nymph.

Every trout stream insect has a Latin or scientific name, and one may often hear other anglers using these names during a hatch. While it is not entirely necessary to know Latin names to catch fish, Latin names eliminate confusion about insect hatches when the fishing action heats up and quick decisions need to be made. For example, there are two mayfly species, *Ephemerella attenuta* and *Ephemerella cornata* that are almost identical to the casual observer but not to the trout; differentiation is the key to its survival.

These multiple hatches can be difficult to unravel, so expect a few failures but don't get discouraged. One of the most satisfying aspects of fly-fishing is its complexity. If success was always a guarantee, then we wouldn't appreciate those moments when, having initially failed, we deduce the problem, apply the appropriate correction, and catch that elusive trout.

EIGHT

The Role of Lake Geology and Ecology in Fly-Fishing

ALTHOUGH MANY FLY ANGLERS ARE STREAM AFI-
cionados, the unique appeal and challenges of lakes should not
be overlooked with regard to fly-fishing opportunities. Part of
the reason some anglers avoid lakes is that fly-fishing is generally a shallow-water activity, effective to a depth of approximately 30 feet. Even fishing at depths of only 20 feet there
is a lot of effort involved in both retrieving the line for casting and searching a relatively large area with numerous casts.
But in the British Isles and Ireland, fly-fishing in still waters
is a long-standing tradition. From the lochs of Scotland to the
lakes of Wales and loughs of Ireland, anglers have historically
pursued trout and salmon alike. T. C. Iven's book, *Stillwater
Flyfishing* (1952), was the first guide to popularize this type of
fishing—a method barely practiced outside the British Isles
at the time of its publication. Though most anglers will target shallow-feeding fish such as bass and panfish, under the
right environmental conditions trout can be taken near the
surface with a fly. But to have consistent success within a lake,
the angler is ultimately going to have to understand the physical structure of a lake and the needs of trout in a lake and be
willing to do a little "prospecting" with regard to locating
trout. Since trout favor certain areas of a lake depending upon
their temperature and oxygen regime, food supply, availability of cover, and spawning sites, being knowledgeable in these
matters before fishing can save a lot of time and energy.

Knowledge of the formation and history of a lake is important to understanding its structure—size, shape, and depth
of a lake basin. In the United States, there are three major areas

with abundant natural lakes: the limestone sinkholes of Florida, the glaciated landscapes of the Midwest region, and the alpine lakes of the Pacific Northwest. Since the focus of this book is on salmonids and their preference for colder water, the emphasis is on the latter two regions. In both of these areas glaciers played the dominant role in lake formation: continental glaciers in the Midwest and alpine (mountain) glaciers along the Continental Divide range. These lakes were formed in the late Pleistocene by the Wisconsin glaciation that covered vast areas of North America.

In Minnesota alone, there are more than 12,000 lakes larger than 10 acres in size. The relentless gouging by the glaciers into the soft bedrock during the last Ice Age created natural depressions or impoundments. Upon the retreat of the glaciers, these basins filled with water, becoming our modern-day Midwest lakes. Forming in mountainous topography like the Sierra Nevada Mountains, a *tarn* is a lake that is found in a cirque—an amphitheater-like area surrounded by high, steep-sided cliffs. Not all cirques contain tarns, since there must be a depression in the bedrock that ultimately filled with glacial meltwater. In contrast, glaciers carving out a U-shaped valley bed of variable rock hardness formed paternoster lakes. As the glacier moves down the valley, basins are created in the weaker rock, and water accumulates after the glacier retreats. The name *paternoster* refers to a string of rosary beads or, in this case, a string of small lakes spread out across a valley but "strung together" by streams or rapids that run between them. The altitude of these lakes appears to be the key variable determining the vitality of the trout population in these lakes. Alpine lakes above eight or nine thousand feet have a short ice-free season and low biological productivity with regard to plant growth (Hughes 1991). While the first factor limits the time the trout can feed, the second factor translates into a lack of food for the trout. Anglers willing to trek up to these lakes will generally find a population of small trout. But as Luscombe (1998) points out, during the heat of late summer, lower-elevation lakes may be too warm for the trout, and therefore anglers should target these high-altitude lakes. With a decrease in altitude comes a corresponding decrease in vertical relief of the surrounding watershed. As with streams, the nature of the watershed plays a critical role in the biological richness of a lake, and generally healthier and bigger trout populations are found in these lower lakes.

A typical lake can be portioned into three distinct spatial zones, each with different physical and biological characteristics that present different opportunities for the trout and angler alike. The *littoral zone* is the relatively shallow near-shore area in which a profusion of macrophytes may be in evidence. They may take the form of floating (water lily, duckweed), emergent (cattail, bulrush), or submergent (stonewort, bladderwort) vegetation. In shallow, clear lakes macrophytes may represent most of the green plant material that is present. But if the lake bottom is too rocky or sandy, these plants cannot establish a foothold to root.

These higher-order plants are vital to the overall health of the biological communities in the lake in that they provide for some essential needs: a food source, a substrate for invertebrates, and a habitat for fish and other organisms. With regard to the first point, since plant matter is a food source for aquatic insects and insects are on the menu of trout, the littoral zone is where trout will spend most of their time during the lake's productive seasons. Obviously, this is the region that should receive the bulk of angling time.

The open-water habitat of lakes includes the limnetic and profundal zones of the water column. The limnetic zone is the area beyond which rooted plants grow and extends vertically to the depth of maximum sunlight penetration. As we will see in a later chapter, this depth can be variable depending primarily upon water clarity. The open-water plant community consists of many species of microscopic floating plants—phytoplankton. While the littoral zone may be rich in insect life, the only aquatic insect found within the limnetic zone is a small floating midge *(Chaoborus)*. Trout are found in the limnetic zone during periods of this insect hatch, also feeding (mainly rainbows) on planktonic organisms and cruising in searching of bigger prey, such as minnows. From the angler's perspective, the limnetic zone is generally not as productive as the littoral zone but may yield bigger trout that have gorged themselves on the large baitfish.

The profundal zone is the deeper, and generally cooler, water below the depth of light penetration. One of the major factors limiting the presence of trout within this area is the lack of any readily available food source. Due to the absence of photosynthesis within this zone, plant growth and its attendant insect community is absent. Another negative factor is that dissolved oxygen may be in short supply due to bacterial decomposition of organic matter that sinks down from the sunlit layers. This zone simply does not satisfy two essential needs of the trout—food and oxygen.

While most glacially formed lakes will be deep enough to have both a limnetic and profundal zone, many ponds are very shallow and have macrophytes throughout their area. These shallow waters can be great trout fisheries if they don't become too hot and evolve into warm-water fisheries. With an abundant supply of food in these lakes readily available to the trout, the potential for trout to grow large in these biologically rich waters is high.

Upon first viewing a lake, many anglers form the impression that a lake is a homogenous mass of water, analogous to a bathtub that is well mixed throughout its volume. Nothing could be further from the truth in that lakes are extremely heterogeneous in their physical (temperature, light levels), chemical (nutrients, contaminants), and biological (aquatic life) characteristics. This variability occurs both on spatial scales, particularly with regard to depth, and on temporal scales ranging from minutes to seasons. The fly angler who recognizes the intrinsic variability of lakes increases the chances of having a successful outing. For example, knowing the vertical temperature structure of a lake and its seasonal change can improve the angler's chance of locating fish within the water column. Let's take a look at this temporal progression.

SPRING. In the early part of this season, just before the ice melts, the water temperature just below the ice will be approximately 32°F and will increase to 39°F near the lake's bottom. This result reflects the fact that fresh water reaches its maximum density at 39°F. (See Technical Focus section below for an explanation.)

As the weather warms, the thermal and density characteristics of the lake change dramatically—the surface water heats up, and consequently its density increases. Ultimately, the surface water warms to 39°F and thus has the same temperature and density as the bottom layer. At this stage, very little wind is needed to mix the lake completely from top to bottom. This spring turnover results in a temperature profile that shows little change with depth. With the lengthening days of March, the surface water temperature will continue to rise, and the strong, gusty winds of this month will continue the mixing (fig. 28). During this warming period, temperature is generally not a limiting factor for the trout, but the availability of food may determine where the angler should concentrate her efforts.

While fish may be found cruising the limnetic zone in search of food, a more likely spot to find the fish is in the biologically productive littoral zone. Targeting these fish calls for a fly line that gets the fly down to the level where the fish are feeding. In order for a line to sink, its density must be greater than that of the water. Manufacturers achieve this by adding lead or tungsten to the line's coating. These lines have various sinking rates from intermediate (1.25 to 1.75 inches per second) to very fast-sinking (7 to 10 inches per second). Though all full-sinking lines are best suited to fishing in still waters, the angler should be aware that each line is designed for a particular situation or environment. For example, if the submerged plants are two to three feet deep, an intermediate line will keep the fly just above the tops of the vegetation. Deeper plants or bottom drop-offs require a faster sinking rate.

SUMMER. As a result of the sun's intense rays and long days, the upper layer of a lake will warm considerably. The temperature differences between the upper and lower layers of the lake will become more pronounced as summer progresses. At this stage, deep lakes are physically stratified into three distinct thermal layers: epilimnion, metalimnion, and hy-

FIG. 28. Seasonal change in lake temperature

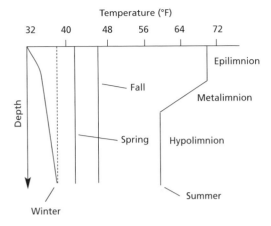

polimnion (fig. 28). The epilimnion is the upper, warm layer and, because it is well mixed, the temperature will not vary appreciably with depth. The depth of this layer depends in part on the degree of wind mixing, but it is most related to lake size. For example, small to moderate-sized lakes (50 to 1,000 acres) have an epilimnion depth of 10 to 25 feet. In contrast, large lakes (larger than 10,000 acres) may be well mixed to a depth of 30 to 50 feet. Below this relatively warm layer is the metalimnion—a layer in which the temperature decreases rapidly with depth. The hypolimnion is the deep, cold layer of the lake. The thermal stratification that is present in the lake during the summer essentially isolates the hypolimnion from the epilimnion. In other words, there is no mixing between the upper and bottom layers of a lake for several months during the summer. In a deep, large lake the difference in temperature from top to bottom is on the order of 36°F. During a hot summer day, trout will generally seek the cooler, deeper waters below the epilimnion and not rise to the surface seeking out prey. An angler intent on pursuing fish during this period should consider using a line with the highest sink rate. However, if the depth of the epilimnion is beyond about 25 feet, even these lines may not be adequate to reach the fish. A better bet is to wait until dusk, since the trout become more active and may even move into the shallower waters to feed. The decreasing surface water temperature and the protection provided by the encroaching darkness afford ample opportunity for the trout to forage successfully.

AUTUMN. As the air temperature drops during autumn, the mixed upper layer will cool, albeit slowly because of the high heat retention property of water, and the density between it and the hypolimnion will decrease. As the season progresses, further cooling of the surface water will result in sinking of this water and a complete overturning or mixing from top to bottom. Most of the water column is isothermal (fig. 28) with a temperature slightly above 39°F. Angling strategies with regard to locating fish are very similar to those applied in the spring. However, the fish that might be caught will probably be bigger than their counterparts in the spring because they have had all of the summer months to gorge themselves on various food items.

WINTER. As the days grow shorter and air temperatures colder, the surface temperature will cool to 32°F, and the lake will again stratify, since the densest water (39°F) is again at that bottom (fig. 28). As we will discuss in greater detail in a later chapter, the cold-water temperatures will effectively shut down the feeding mechanisms of the fish, reduce its food supply, and cause it to seek the relatively warmer bottom layer. This is the time to put away the fly rod and start restocking the fly collection in anticipation of the spring thaw.

In summary, this pattern—spring turnover, summer stratification, autumn turnover, and winter stratification—is typical of temperate lakes and is generally absent in tropical lakes. Lakes that exhibit two mixing periods during the year are referred to as *dimictic*. While this pattern is common in most deep lakes, shallow lakes may not stratify in the summer or may only partially stratify for a short period, since the wind-mixing results in a uniform temperature profile with regard to depth. During these two turnover periods, trout are most active but tend to confine their feeding to the plant-rich shallow areas of a lake. In comparison, during the summer doldrums, trout generally seek the comfort of the cooler water found within the deeper reaches of the lake.

Since the beginning of the twentieth century, lakes have been classified according to their *trophic* state—a specified level of nutrition. A eutrophic (well-nourished) lake has a high concentration of nutrients and abundant plant growth—most in the form of tiny plants such as algae. Eutrophic lakes have watersheds with rich organic soils or heavily fertilized agricultural regions that enrich the lake with the nutrients (nitrates and phosphates) that stimulate plant growth.

When nutrients are plentiful in an aquatic system, algae multiply explosively, discoloring the water shades of green and brown with their pigments. These blooms significantly increase the amount of organic matter in the aquatic ecosystem. Though plants are intrinsic to the vitality of the ecosystem, a heavy bloom of short-lived algae ultimately results in die-off and subsequent sinking to the bottom. And there is the crux of the problem: the bottom-dwelling bacteria that decompose this dead organic matter consume oxygen. In a hypereutrophic lake, because the plant growth is so abundant, the decay rate is high in the hypolimnion, causing oxygen to be depleted. During the summer, because the lake is strongly stratified, eutrophic lakes may show a complete loss of dissolved oxygen (anoxic condition) within the hypolimnion. Clearly, fish and most other organisms cannot survive within the hypolimnion of such lakes. But warm-water fish that can live in the epilimnion will often be abundant in these lakes. Bass, panfish, carp, and bullheads often thrive in a highly eutrophic lake.

Another oxygen-related problem in eutrophic lakes is winterkill—fish mortality resulting from insufficient oxygen in a frozen lake. The ice that forms on the lake surface during the winter isolates the upper layer of the lake from the atmosphere. Since the transfer of oxygen from the atmosphere to the water is interrupted, dissolved oxygen concentrations may become depleted in the presence of bacterial decomposition of organic matter. The resultant fish kill is not all negative, since it may lead to a better fishery for the angler and also to improved water quality. One theory proposes that the hardier fish that survive the winterkill will have less competition for food during the spring thaw, so their rate of growth will accelerate, and they will attain a larger size. Since biologists have shown that the smaller fish are more susceptible to the effects of the winterkill, fewer small fish reduces the predation on algae-eating organisms. Left unmolested, these organisms can graze upon the algae and significantly reduce their impact within the lake.

At the other end of the trophic spectrum are oligotrophic lakes that have a small amount of nutrients and are biologically unproductive with regard to plant growth and abundance. Because of the relatively small amount of organic matter that decays in an oligotrophic lake, the hypolimnion is not depleted of its supply of oxygen. In this case, the lack of oxygen does not prevent organisms from inhabiting the hypolimnion. For example, since lake trout require cold, clear, well-oxygenated water, they are found almost exclusively in oligotrophic lakes. In summer, they may spend most of their time in the hypolimnion since they prefer temperatures from 39°F to 48°F, but in the spring and fall they can be found at relatively shallow depths. Extremely deep oligotrophic lakes like Lake Superior (1,000 ft) and Lake Tahoe (1,640 ft) will have an oxygenated hypolimnion throughout the year, since they are essentially mixed all winter and spring. But within the hypolimnion of many moderately deep lakes (maximum depth about 170 ft) anoxic conditions may develop during the summer. Interestingly, limnologists will still categorize these lakes as oligotrophic because of their low nutrient input and low plant concentration. During the summer, these lakes exhibit a two-story fishery—an upper warm-water fishery overlying a deeper cold-water salmonid fishery. This cold-water fishery is very sensitive to nutrient input and increased algae production, since these factors will accelerate the rate of oxygen depletion in the hypolimnion during the summer.

Many lakes fall between the above two trophic extremes and are referred to as mesotrophic (middle-nourished) lakes. These lakes have an adequate nutrient supply that supports good plant growth. The main vegetative assemblages that define mesotrophic lakes are the submerged rooted water plants such as shore weed, alternate flowered water milfoil, and small

TABLE 5. Physical, chemical, and biological characteristics of various lakes

Characteristics	Oligotrophic Lakes	Mesotrophic Lakes	Eutrophic Lakes
Depth	Deep	Medium	Shallow
Volume	Large	Medium	Small
Nutrient amount	Low	Low to medium	High
Productivity	Low	Medium	High
Flora	Macrophytes	Macrophytes	Algae, macrophytes
Fish	Salmonids	Salmonids, pike	Sunfish, carp
Dissolved oxygen	High	Variable	Low
Examples	Lake Tahoe	Lake Champlain	Lake Okeechobee

pondweed. Table 5 summarizes the salient characteristics of these different types of lakes.

Many lakes will undergo a process of ecological succession, aging from a young oligotrophic lake to an older eutrophic lake. This process of eutrophication, the progress of a lake toward a eutrophic condition, is often discussed in terms of lake history—the changing of a lake over a period of time. As a result of nutrient-loading, organic matter input, and bacterial decomposition, lakes will change in structure, generally becoming shallower, and in biological makeup with increased concentration of algae. While all lakes exhibit some degree of succession, this concept of lake aging has unfortunately been interpreted by some as an inevitable process leading to the eventual "death" of a lake. In fact, many oligotrophic lakes, like Lake Tahoe, have not changed appreciably since the last glaciation because of their favorable topography, watershed characteristics, and lake morphology. With regard to the latter point, shallow lakes are likely to age faster than deep lakes because they generally do not stratify, allowing nutrients to remain in circulation and readily available for plants. In addition, because of their smaller volume, nutrient-loading from the watershed will have a greater impact.

With so much physical and geological difference among lakes, it should not be surprising that the fish themselves vary greatly. This is the result of several interacting factors: the water quality, the presence or absence of particular food items, the ecological niches within the lake and the behavior of trout within these niches, and the genetic makeup of the trout. In addition to the vertical temperature structure within a lake, one of the defining differences between still-water environments and streams is the absence of a current. Unlike stream trout, which are dependent upon the flow of water to transport the food items to them and can remain relatively stationary, lake trout must move in search of their food. The vast majority of the trout will cruise the shallow lake margins. Here they are likely to find plant growth and the aquatic animals that feed on and reside within the plants. Some lakes have a large population of crustaceans such as freshwater shrimp and crayfish. Such a diet provides a high level of carotenoids—the orange-red pigment found in these crustaceans—that is responsible for the vivid red or pink markings of the fins and the "salmon-pink" flesh color. (I suppose the saying "You are what you eat" is also applicable to fish.) When there is little in the way of crustacean food items, the diet consists of either insects (predominantly damselflies and dragonflies) or small baitfish, and the fish are more muted in their skin and flesh coloration. The key point for the fly angler to remember about these food items is that, since they have mobility, the angler must impart motion to the fly to make it appear realistic to the fish. Since you don't have the current to help you, once the fly has settled on the surface, you should "strip line" to impart a series of stop-and-go movements to the fly. The darting motion of the fly resembles a prey attempting to escape from becoming an easy meal for a hungry predator.

While holding is the modus operandi of stream-dwelling fish, cruising is the name of the game for still-water fish. Rainbow trout always cruise, whether they are feeding or abstaining, and so do many other lake species. This perpetual motion may be partially in response to the physiological need to augment its oxygen supply by forcing oxygen-enriched water over its gills through locomotion. Known as ram ventilation, the fish literally swims with its mouth open, and its forward motion allows for the flow of water. For some fish, like mackerel, ram ventilation is mandatory—if they stop moving they suffocate. Other fish, like trout, switch from active brachial pumping to ram ventilation as the dissolved oxygen decreases in the lake. While the stream angler is taught to focus in, look for holding fish, and mentally catalog subsurface features, the still-water angler must have a broader, more encompassing view in response to the fish moving from place to place.

The problem may be even more intimidating in large lakes where it is possible to find trout in several different niches. Some of the trout might patrol the weed lines of the littoral zone, others position themselves at the mouths of in-flowing streams, and still others cruise the limnetic zone. But this behavior of the trout is directly linked to their feeding preferences and habits. Some trout, like rainbows, feed predominantly upon zooplankton (tiny to small weakly swimming animals) in the open deep water, particularly during the summer. Because zooplankton often occur in localized high concentrations, the trout will tend to congregate together, or school, since the larger numbers improve the chance of locating the food. In contrast, baitfish-eating trout tend to be solitary, having greater success at hunting on schools of baitfish individually than as a group. The majority of the trout will focus on consuming a wide variety of invertebrate food items from the shallow lake margins. In order to achieve success, they form loose associations or schools and will cover vast areas in search of insects and crustaceans.

But the trout are not locked into this feeding pattern, since most lake trout will change their behavior during the year, or even from day to day. During the early spring, zooplankton abundance is low, and trout will concentrate on the more productive lake margins. As the zooplankton population increases dramatically in the spring in response to the lake turnover, trout may abandon the margins for the zooplankton pastures. But even these trout may be tempted away from the deep-residing zooplankton if Mother Nature presents them with another opportunity, such as an evening fall of insects on the water surface or a heavy thunderstorm resulting in the formation of insect-carrying feeder streams. In the latter case, trout will move into these temporary rivulets and take up lies like river trout. The angler who fishes a lake needs to be flexible to meet the changing conditions and prepared with an assortment of floating and sinking flies to match the trout's dietary preference.

How does all this information about the geology and ecology of lakes translate into the trout "hot spots"? Since all fish relate in one way or another to shelter or cover, I can't overemphasize its importance in locating fish. Trout must have shelter, both from predators and from direct sunlight, so they always will be either next to or within easy access of shelter. Places to probe with a fly include submerged logs and limbs, drop-offs, and weed beds. As in streams, the woody debris that may be found along a lake shoreline provides cover for the wary trout. Drop-offs occur wherever there is a marked change in the gradient of the lake bottom. In particular, the transition between the littoral and limnetic zone is often marked by a significant increase in depth. Trout will intuitively seek the darkness of this deeper water. When we refer to weed beds, we are essentially targeting the area of submerged aquatic vegetation in the littoral zone. A trout seeking cover will often rest over the weed bed for the protective camouflage it provides— dark trout over a dark substrate.

Locating a food source means finding trout. On a windy day, fish that part of the lake where debris and surface food (midges, floating insects) are being concentrated into a line by the wind. These lines, called windrows, are oriented parallel to the wind direction, and trout can often be found cruising these lines, feeding on the trapped insects. Also, try areas next to inlet and outlet streams, because they are a ready supply of terrestrial and aquatic insects and also have concentrations of baitfish around their mouths. Since only a few food items that trout target are independent of the near-shore rooted aquatic vegetation, this is an area that should receive considerable angling attention. As pointed out by Hughes (1991), though this vegetation may be a direct source of food for foraging insects, its primary function is as a surface for the attachment of periphyton—microscopic algae that form a green slime on the vegetative surface. The large surface area provided by the tangle of roots, stems, and leaf structures provide ample platforms for the attachment of this algae. This profusion of periphyton growth is then grazed upon by a host of invertebrates that subsequently attract hungry trout. Thus, a basic ecological principle that should be committed to memory is that organisms go where there is food and, as an angler, so should you!

Lakes that have a self-sustaining population of brown and rainbow trout must also have adequate spawning sites. In particular, the main requirement of these trout for spawning is moving water. In a lake environment, this necessitates the existence of an inlet stream. Depending upon the time of year (see chapter 10), trout will gather around the mouths of these feeder streams in anticipation of spawning. At the mouths of these streams, there is often a deep channel where trout can hide before moving upstream. A nymph or streamer fished on a weighted line will often take trout in these channels. In the absence of an inlet stream, brook trout can adapt by using gravel beds as spawning sites. Because of this high degree of flexibility, brook trout is probably the only trout species that has the potential to overpopulate a lake, leading to severe strains on existing food resources and ultimately a stunted population.

Does size matter? I think many fly anglers would answer in the affirmative when it comes to trout. If size is important, how does trout size vary from one lake to the next? Research has shown that there can be considerable variability in the size of trout that inhabit lakes. Fish measurements (length of fish from tip of snout to tail) of brown trout from a dozen lakes in the British Isles showed that the largest fish sampled was almost three times the size of the smallest fish. But what biological and physical variables, environmental conditions, and lake types are most likely to yield that trophy trout? This is an age-old question that fisheries biologists have attempted to unravel for years. Let's take a look at the most current scientific opinion on this topic.

One common theory holds that fish size generally decreases with increasing latitude. Greenhalgh (1997) points out that there is little validity to this theory, since some Alaskan lakes yield larger trout than lakes in the Rockies; and, in continental Europe, some alpine lakes produce smaller trout than lakes in northern Norway and Sweden. Other arguments point to the role that genetics play in determining size. Support for this argument comes from the classic case study of the cutthroat trout that occupied Pyramid Lake in the beginning part of the twentieth century. Pyramid Lake, which is located in the desert area of western Nevada, yielded a record trout of 41 pounds that was caught by John Skimmerhorn in 1925. Though this official record still stands today, anecdotal evidence points to even larger fish, probably topping 60 pounds, that may have been caught by the local Native Americans. Because of the success of this native trout, the lake was stocked with other strains of trout, but they never attained comparable success, leading to the conclusion that they lacked the appropriate genetic makeup for rapid and sustained growth.

However, recently a number of private enterprises in both Europe and North America have been engaged in raising genetically modified trout and salmon. By implanting a growth hormone in the fish, the growth rate has been accelerated by a factor of four to six times faster than that found in natural fish. Though the initial intent is to bring marketable-sized fish to the consumer quicker, there has been some discussion about introducing these "super" fish into the aquatic environment to create "trophy" lakes. There is concern within the environmental community over the risks that these modified fish might pose on the indigenous population. In particular, these efficient, fast-growing fish may outcompete the native species for specific resources and habitats. In addition, the release of these engineered fish might harm the genetic diversity of the wild species, through the release of many similar genomes. Though these are valid pragmatic concerns, I propose another claim that has been articulated by a number of philosophers: much of nature's value derives from its being naturally evolved. We "value" our lake primarily because it is natural, wild, unaltered, untouched by the hand of man. We accept all of its "warts" and seek these places as respites from the ever-encroaching artificial world. Would knowing that a part of our aquatic world has been altered or modified by human intervention detract from our enjoyment and overall relationship with nature?

While having the appropriate genes certainly does influence growth rates in some cases in nature, the pendulum of opinion is swinging toward the environment of the fish being more important than its heredity in determining size. One of the key environmental variables determining why some lakes produce bigger trout than others is the biological productivity of the lake, or its ability to support a vibrant community of green algae. In some lakes where macrophytes are absent, these plants may be the main group of biological producers—photosynthetic organisms. The importance of these plants lies in the fact that they are at the base of a lake's food chain; that is, the number of mouths food passes through on the way to the top predator. Phytoplankton are fed upon by herbivores (such as zooplankton), the vegetarians of the aquatic community, which in turn are eaten by the consumers. In most lakes, the top-level consumer is the trout. Consumers often shift food levels throughout their life cycle in response to their changing growth and metabolic needs. For example, a larval fish may feed directly on the phytoplankton but switch and feed on larger herbivores and ultimately prey upon smaller fish as it reaches maturity. Research has shown that the length of the food chain is the critical factor in determining trout size. In general, the longer the food chain, the bigger the fish. Note in figure 29 that, while the sport fish may feed directly on the herbivores, feeding upon the prey fish yields greater growth rates in the fish. If the trout chooses the latter food pathway, there are then a total of four levels/links to the food chain. But not all lakes exhibit these relatively long food chains. A survey of aquatic life from the Great Lakes to small ponds by ecologists at Cornell University found that the food-chain length is determined by the size of the lake. Their results showed that larger lakes have longer food chains than smaller lakes, though the research did not pinpoint the specific cause and effect.

FIG. 29. Typical lake food chain

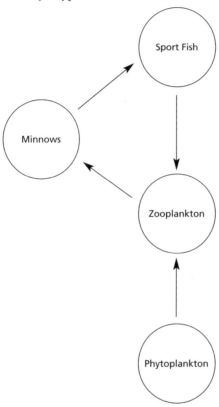

But what does all this research and study about lake environments, trophic levels, and food chains boil down to with regard to yielding big fish? The angler targeting size over numbers of fish would increase the chance of success by focusing on moderately productive lakes that can support an abundant population of baitfish; in other words, a relatively large mesotrophic lake. A baitfish imitation, like a streamer fished on a sinking line to reach the deep, cruising fish, may be just the ticket to put that smile on your face.

Technical Focus

Most of us realize that the chemical expression for water, H_2O, means that a molecule of water is composed of 2 atoms of hydrogen and 1 atom of oxygen. The combination of these atoms is in the form of a dipole structure, with each hydrogen atom possessing a single positive charge and the oxygen atom a double negative charge. This dipole structure causes the attraction of another water molecule. This electrostatic attachment, called hydrogen-bonding, produces clusters of water molecules. At 39°F the water molecules are tightly packed together in a lattice structure. Below 39°F, the molecules move slightly apart and create a more open lattice structure (less volume and density).

NINE

Aquatic Optics: From the Perspective of the Angler and Fish

THAT BRIGHT SPRING DAY HAS LURED YOU TO YOUR favorite stream to test your skills against its wily inhabitants. Approaching the stream, the sunlight glare from the water surface causes you reflexively to squint against this incoming light. Though it's uncomfortable, you're here to locate fish. While peering beneath the water surface, you question whether that is a fish lurking near a rock or simply a submerged branch. Further thought leads you to ponder the limits of the visual acuity of fish in their watery environment. Can they detect my tiny mayfly imitation? Can they differentiate colors? Are certain species better suited to visually detecting prey and predator compared to other species? The sight of another angler crouching down as he approaches the stream interrupts your train of thought. Why has a fellow fly angler assumed this low profile? In order to answer these questions and learn of other optical phenomena, we need to begin our discussion with a basic understanding of the energy emitted from the sun.

The energy transferred from the sun to the water surface is called radiant energy, or radiation. It travels in the form of waves that have both electrical and magnetic properties—hence electromagnetic waves. Other examples of electromagnetic waves include radio and microwaves. All of these waves can be distinguished from one another by their wavelengths. Like water waves that travel over the ocean surface, some electromagnetic waves are relatively short and some long. For example, the sun emits radiation in the form of visible light that has a wavelength of about one-millionth of an inch (microinch)—a distance of less than one-hundredth the diameter of a strand of hair. In comparison television and radio waves have wavelengths of 3 and 330 feet respectively. Approximately 44 percent of the sun's emitted radiation is in the form of visible light, the remainder divided between ultraviolet and infrared radiation that have wavelengths shorter and longer than visible light, respectively. But why is the emission confined to this relatively narrow band? Though we don't need to go into detail here, the wavelengths of emitted radiation from an object is a function of the object's temperature. Essentially, very hot objects, like the sun (whose surface temperatures approach thousands of degrees), emit most of their radiation as visible light. The energy associated with each type of radiation increases as the wavelength decreases. The sunburn that an unwary angler receives results from the relatively high energy content of ultraviolet radiation compared to visible radiation.

While our eyes cannot detect all forms of electromagnetic radiation, they are sensitive to radiation in the visible portion of the radiation spectrum—1.6 to 2.7 microinches. Specifically, these waves stimulate antennae-like nerve endings in the retina of the eye. These antennas are of two types—rods and cones. The rods respond to all the wavelengths of visible light and allow us to distinguish light from dark. The cones respond to specific wavelengths of radiation between 1.6 (color violet) and 2.7 (red) microinches. The cones fire an impulse through the nervous system to the brain, allowing us to perceive this impulse as the sensation of color. Thus the cones permit us to distinguish the lateral pink band of the rainbow trout from its dark spots. Radiation wavelengths shorter than 1.6 microinches or longer than 2.7 microinches do not stimulate color sensation in the human eye. If all visible wavelengths strike the cones of the eye with equal intensity, then the composite of these wavelengths is white light. The noonday sun appears white to us because all visible wavelengths reach the eyes' cones. Correspondingly, a setting sun may be blood red, since only the longer red wavelengths are reaching our eyes.

But why does a fish, a fly, or an angler's hat have color even though none of these is hot enough to produce radiation at visible wavelengths? We can see the vivid orange underside of a wild brook trout because all other colors of the visible spectrum have been absorbed except orange. Only the orange light is returned from the underside of the trout to our eyes. The green rim of a hat returns the color green to the observer's eyes since it absorbs all visible wavelengths except green. A dark-colored fish—let's say black in appearance—absorbs all visible wavelengths and returns no light at all. Since no radiation strikes the cones or rods, the surface of the fish appears black.

When a light wave strikes an object or surface, what happens to it depends on the energy of the light wave, the natural frequency at which electrons vibrate within the material, and the strength with which these atoms in the material hold onto their electrons. One of the most basic phenomenons that result when light hits a surface is reflection. A reflected wave always bounces off the surface at an angle equal to the angle at which the incident wave strikes the surface. Reflection occurs because the atoms in some materials hold onto their electrons loosely, and these electrons are free to move from one atom to another. The incident light ray energizes these electrons, and they simply send this energy back out of the surface as a light wave with the same frequency of the incident wave. For example, most metals have loosely held electrons, so these metals reflect visible light and appear to be shiny.

The amount of light reflected from the water surface is in part dependent upon the angle at which the sun's rays strike the surface. When the sun is directly overhead, only 2 percent of the incident light is reflected, with most of the light penetrating the water column. With the sun low on the horizon, approximately 85 percent of the light is reflected from the water surface, hence limiting the angler's ability to see below the water surface. But what exactly is glare? The brightness or intensity of light is measured in lumens—the unit of measurement in physics to determine the degree of luminosity. If you are indoors tying some flies or reading fly-fishing catalogues, the intensity of the artificial light source is approximately 400 to 600 lumens. While fly-fishing on a sunny day, the brightness may range from about 1,000 lumens in the shade to more than 6,000 lumens on an open stretch of water.

Our eyes are comfortable until the light intensity increases to approximately 3,500 lumens. When the brightness of the reflected light reaches about 4,000 lumens, our eyes begin to experience difficulty dealing with this increased intensity. What we see when we try to look at these brighter areas are flashes of silvery-white, or glare. The following explanation may be a bit esoteric, but hopefully you will see its relevance. Visible light is unpolarized when the electric field vectors of this electromagnetic radiation are randomly oriented as viewed parallel to the direction of light propagation. Polarization results when the field vectors have a preferred orientation. If the electric field vectors are in a single plane, the light is linearly polarized. Etienne Louis Malus discovered in 1809 that light can be partially or completely polarized by reflection. When sunlight is reflected from the water surface, the light is polarized in the plane of the surface, hence horizontally polarized. This reflected polarized light is glare. When the eye receives too much reflected light, it involuntarily closes the iris. Once it has closed the iris as far as it can, the eye then responds by squinting.

The angler who invests in a pair of polarized sunglasses easily alleviates sun glare. Polarizing sunglasses allow only the vertical component of light to pass through; the horizontal component is blocked out, which reduces the glare. This is accomplished by means of a polarizing film applied to a transparent plastic or glass surface. The chemical compound used will typically be composed of molecules that vertically align in relation to each other. When applied to the lens, the molecules create a microscopic filter that blocks any light not matching this alignment. Polarizing sunglasses are as valuable as a quality fly rod to the angler, since they make seeing into the water much easier, improving contrast and increasing your comfort level when out in the sun. How can you determine if your current sunglasses are polarized? One simple method is to view the water surface with your current glasses. If the glasses are polarized, the brightness of the water surface will change as you tilt your head from the horizontal to the vertical plane. When your head is horizontal, the surface looks dimmer, since the polarizing filter lets through just the vertically vibrating light. The reflection looks brighter as you tilt your head, since the horizontal polarized light is now let through.

The shade of color or tint of the glasses that you choose should be considered from more than just a cosmetic perspective. Tinting determines the parts of the light spectrum that are absorbed by the lens. Manufacturers use different colors to produce specific results depending upon the nature of the outdoor activity. From an angling perspective, gray-tinted glasses are a good choice, since they reduce the overall amount of brightness and glare but with the least amount of color distortion. The latter point is particularly important to the angler trying to match the color of a particular natural insect with a selection from the fly box. Yellow tints reduce the amount of blue light while allowing a larger percentage of other wavelengths through. Since blue light tends to bounce off a lot of objects in the atmosphere, it can create a kind a glare known as *blue haze*. Since the yellow tint virtually eliminates the blue portion of the light spectrum, it has the effect of making objects sharp and enhancing their contrast. The downside to this tint is that it really distorts color perception. Amber and brownish tints are also good general-purpose tints in that they increase contrast and clarity. These tints also have the advantage of absorbing short wavelength radiation such as the color violet and near-ultraviolet radiation. Research has suggested that these wavelengths may contribute to the formation of eye cataracts over time. But, similar to yellow lenses, there is significant color distortion. I know what you're thinking next. What about those rose-colored glasses? This tint offers the best contrast of objects against either a green or blue background. So obviously this tint could provide some advantage in viewing floating objects against either a blue or green water surface. But you may have to deal with the ridicule from other not-so-fashion-conscious fly anglers.

One final component that should be considered in purchasing sunglasses is their ability to filter the ultraviolet (UV) rays. A number of serious eye problems are attributed to the eye's exposure to UV rays. UV radiation is divided into two components based on wavelength: UV-A and UV-B. As a protective mechanism, the cornea of the eye absorbs all of the UV-B and most of the UV-A. But prolonged exposure to this radiation over time can lead to cataracts. Also, the small amount of the UV-A that gets past your cornea can lead to macular degeneration, the leading cause of blindness in older people. On the extreme end of exposure to UV radiation, the eyes may develop either a cancer or photokeratitis, literally sunburn of the retina. In summary, quality sunglasses will probably not only improve your angling skills but also protect your health so that you can practice improving your skills.

In addition to light being reflected from the water surface, sunlight can also be scattered—the dispersion of light in all different directions. The blue color of your favorite pristine alpine lake or the greenish color of a Florida bass lake both result from the scattering of sunlight. Let's see how this works. Light is scattered by such objects as water molecules, microscopic plants, and sediment particles. Water molecules are many times more effective at scattering blue light than red light. This type of selective scattering, formally referred to as *Rayleigh scattering,* holds when the scattering particles are small compared to the wavelength of light. In crystal-clear, transparent lakes the blue surface color results because the only scattering agents are the water molecules. A deeper blue means simply that a greater percentage of the scattered light is the result of Rayleigh scattering.

When the particles are of the same size or larger than the wavelength, the scattering is less dependent upon the wavelength. Eutrophic lakes generally have a large abundance of suspended microscopic plant matter. These scattering agents are large enough to scatter more than one wavelength of visible radiation more or less equally—no wavelength dependence. This type of nonselective scattering, *Mie scattering,* results in the color of the water surface representing a mixture of more than one color. With small concentrations of plant matter the color of the water appears blue-green. As the plant matter increases, the lake may have a pea-soup green appearance. Plants are green because of the chlorophyll in the plant cells. Chlorophyll *a* absorbs mainly blue-violet and red and reflects green; chlorophyll *b* absorbs mainly blue and orange and reflects yellow-green. This process of nonselective scattering attains its most vivid demonstration after an intense rainstorm results in a large influx of sediments into the aquatic environment. These large soil particles are efficient scatterers of multiple wavelengths in the visible spectrum and result in a muddy, chocolate-brown appearance—not your idyllic fly-fishing spot.

While a considerable portion of sunlight striking the water surface may be reflected and scattered, the remainder is transmitted and absorbed as it penetrates the water column. Essentially, water is nearly opaque to light, and the total light intensity decreases with depth. The rate at which light decreases with depth depends upon the amount of dissolved substances (such as organic matter) and suspended materials. With regard to absorption, the frequency of the visible light is very near the vibration frequency of the electrons in the material. The energy of the light rays incites these electrons to start vibrating. When the electrons are held tightly to the atoms, their vibration energy results in the atoms speeding up, colliding with other atoms, and surrendering this energy as heat. Since water is not very transparent to light, it obviously limits the angler's ability to look within the water column, pinpoint holding places, and see the fish. While a mountain creek may run clear for days at a time and allow an angler ample opportunity to sight-cast to even deep-holding fish, there are those periods where these small creeks may be overwhelmed by their sediment load, which limits light penetration. During these extreme conditions it might be difficult for the angler even to see his hand below the surface, never mind that minuscule fly.

The maximum depth at which algae and macrophytes can grow is determined by the light intensity. Biologists estimate this depth to be the point at which the amount of light avail-

TABLE 6. Light penetration as function of eutrophic state

Lake	Eutrophic Zone (ft)	Description
Crater Lake	>390	Ultra-oligotrophic
Lake Superior	160	Oligotrophic
Lake Ontario	65	Mesotrophic
Lake Erie	40	Meso-eutrophic
Halsted Bay (MN)	<3	Eutrophic

able is reduced to approximately 1 percent of the amount available at the surface. This layer of water where sunlight is sufficient for photosynthesis to occur is the euphotic zone. The transparency of lakes is determined mainly by the amount of microscopic plants that will reflect and scatter light and thus limit its vertical transmission. In general, oligotrophic lakes are quite transparent in comparison to eutrophic lakes. Light penetration in the former may be on the order of tens of feet, while limited to less than three feet in the latter (table 6). While a weighted fly attached to a fast-sinking line may be the angler's choice in oligotrophic lakes, the limited visibility afforded the fish in eutrophic lakes may decrease the usefulness of this technique.

To survive, many fish must depend upon their ability to visually detect prey within the water column. In its simplest form, the ability to see for any animal has two components—a way of collecting light and forming an image. In humans, as light enters the cornea of the eye, it bends and, with the aid of a lens, helps to focus an image on the retina. This bending of light occurs as light travels between two objects of different densities—say, the cornea of the eye and air.

While this anatomical setup allows us to see quite well on land, it is essentially useless underwater, since the densities of water and the cornea are quite close in magnitude. Consequently, fish must rely solely on a lens to bend and focus the light into a clear image. The lenses of a fish's eye are perfectly spherical, which allows them to see underwater. They focus by moving the lens in and out, similar to using the focus ring on a camera to move the lens, instead of stretching the lens, common to humans. They cannot dilate or contract their pupils in response to changing light conditions, since the lenses bulge through the iris. As the fish's depth increases and the intensity of light decreases, the eye size increases to gather the dimmer light. Nocturnal foraging fish generally have larger eyes than diurnal fish.

Visually dependent predation is quite common and well developed in the salmonids. But trout and salmon have only fair vision at relatively low light levels. However, compared to the rainbow and brook trout, the retina of the brown trout is better suited to the dim light. This may explain, in part, why, if rainbows and browns cohabit the same stretch of a stream, brown trout will typically be found near dark, undercut banks or submerged structure. They are more comfortable with cover than the rainbow trout, which may forage in open channels. Even though large brown trout have a tendency to feed most heavily at dusk or after dark, they too seem to have difficulty locating a fly at night unless it produces noise or vibration.

When a fish seems to lose interest in a particular colored fly that was successful during the day, it may be due to decreasing light levels or changes in water clarity. Any competent angler should take into account the effect of water clarity and light levels on the selection of flies by their color. To decide when specific fly colors need to be used or avoided, a starting point is to think of color in terms of contrast rather than a particular shade or tint. In clear water and bright light, dark-colored flies that stand out against the lighter background are a good choice. Stained, murky water and/or low light levels require the angler to use light-colored flies that contrast with the dark environment. Any angler should consider using flies that project a strong silhouette against the background light. Some creative flytiers may even add a strip or two of bright silver material to each side of their dressed fly. When retrieved, these flies sparkle and flash because they reflect the subsurface light that hits them. At depths where light levels fall off sharply, these flies can be effective in triggering strikes.

The angler must be flexible and attuned to changing water conditions. If the wind picks up, churning the water surface, and/or a bank of clouds rolls in and decreases light levels, the angler must adjust accordingly with regard to fly selection. In addition, some research has pointed to the fact that water temperature may have an effect on fish vision. These studies have shown that the colder the water, the better the visual acuity of the fish. The rationale is that these colder temperatures facilitate the functioning of the eyes' cells. With other environmental variables being the same, fish should be better able to detect smaller flies at deeper levels in cold water than in warm water.

Not only is there a significant attenuation of light with depth, but also the water and suspended material selectively filter out colors from the visible light spectrum. In very clear water, the first color to be absorbed is red, disappearing in the first 7 feet. As depth increases, colors continue to be filtered out until blue is the last color to be absorbed, penetrating to a depth of 30 feet or more. At this depth the ambient light has a bluish hue. In waters containing moderate to abundant plant growth, both blue and red are filtered quickly within the first 7 feet. The yellow and green colors will penetrate to a depth of approximately 26 feet. Ultra-eutrophic waters, with their very high concentration of plant and organic matter, limit light penetration the most and filter out colors rapidly. Background light appears reddish brown.

Now let's put this information in the context of fishing a particular color of fly. Consider the scenario of a blue-colored fly descending through a clear water column. In the relatively shallow depths its color would still be visible, since only the longer wavelengths have been absorbed. At the depth where the color blue is absorbed, the fly blends into the dark background, becoming essentially invisible to the fish. The same fly descending in muddy water would lose its color very quickly, as the blue wavelengths are filtered out first. The angler should consider the above environments if fishing with a yellow-colored fly.

There has been considerable debate among fly anglers about which color(s) of deceiver flies are most effective in attracting and catching fish. Composed of synthetic hairlike fibers, their overall appearance mimics a particular baitfish. Generally, these flies are two-toned in coloration and cover a myriad of color combinations. Consider a red (top section) and white (bottom section) fly that is fished quite deep with the aid of a sinking line. Recall that with regard to the physics of light attenuation the color red is filtered out quickly, essentially resulting in a dark and white colored fly. While fishing a blue and white deceiver at the same depth would not result in loss of any color, is there really any difference in appearance of the fly to the fish? Can fish really discern subtle changes in coloration? While in certain situations color may trigger an attack by a predator, the consensus of opinion is that color contrast of the fly is the more important factor when fishing deep flies. In the aquatic environment, most fish are darkly colored on their dorsal (top) side and lightly colored on their bottom side. It is postulated that this contrast is a protective adaptation by certain prey fish to their sunlit environment. When viewed from below by a predator, a prey fish will blend in with the lighted surface waters. However, if the situation is reversed, with the predator on top and the prey below, the prey may still have advantage by blending in with the darker background of the deeper waters.

While trout can be opportunistic feeders, they can at times be very selective with regard to their choice of food items. Part of this selectivity is often based upon the color of the natural food item in comparison to that of the fly. For the angler, the question then becomes how close the color match has to be to achieve success. Gary Borger, the noted fly angler and author, has studied this question for a number of years and has concluded that trout can be color sensitive—selecting a brown-colored offering, yet spurning an olive-colored one. But how selective are trout to shades of a particular color? Does the angler need many variations of a basic color (dark green, forest green, heather green) to be successful on a consistent basis? Even though natural food items may vary slightly in coloration, Borger concludes that it would be disadvantageous for trout to be too discriminating with regard to color because too many food items would have to be discarded from their diet. Then there are times on the river when trout, much to the pleasure of all anglers, will strike with abandon at brightly colored flies that have no analogue in nature. These flies, often referred to as *attractors,* may stimulate the feeding instinct in fish. It is also hypothesized that, since the angler also easily sees them, they may inspire confidence in presenting them to the fish. Ultimately, the selection of a fly by its color should not leave an angler flustered and red-faced; keep it simple and experiment.

Another common debate among fly anglers is the selection of a fly line by its color. Some anglers prefer a brightly colored line; arguing that it enhances their ability to see the line on the water and in the air. A yellow or orange line standing out against a blue sky allows the angler to see at all times exactly where the line is going, during both the back and forward cast. Others prefer lines that are more muted in color and blend in with the natural background. Fish see color, they argue, so why spook fish with colors that are not part of their environment? Guides in New Zealand will allow their clients to use only lines that fit in with the natural color scheme, often a dull green. Still others argue that fish will be sent scurrying if they see the fly line regardless of its color and that a long, essentially invisible leader is the key to successful angling.

Remember our crouching streamside angler from the introduction in this chapter? We can now attempt to answer this puzzle by further examination of what happens to light when it hits an object—in this case, the process of refraction. The bending of light, refraction, occurs when light waves penetrate deeply into the material and slow down. This has the effect of bending the light inside the material toward the normal, an imaginary straight line that is oriented perpendicular to the surface of the object. The amount of bending, or the *angle of refraction,* of the light wave depends upon how much light slows down in the material. And how much the light slows down, in part, depends on the density of the material. Diamonds are considerably denser than water and would not have that glitter without the light waves slowing down and

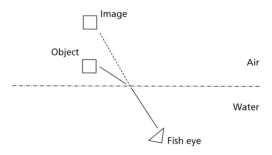

FIG. 30. Displacement of image relative to object due to refraction from the perspective of the fish

bending to a greater degree than in water; that is, they have a higher index of refraction than water. Willebrord Snell, a sixteenth- and seventeenth-century mathematician, discovered the physical law governing refraction and is often considered the father of modern optics. But what does refraction have to do with our angler?

As light enters the water at an angle, it is bent toward the normal. This refraction causes a visual distortion in what the fish sees, essentially making the angler appear to be in a position where he isn't. The refraction occurs only once at the boundary between air and water, and after that the light travels in a straight line—the line of sight. The eye-brain interaction of the fish cannot account for the bending of light. The eye and brain assume the light travels in a straight line and simply extends all incoming light rays back out along this line of sight. In this case, the angler appears to be higher that he actually is because the image of the angler is displaced above the object (fig. 30). The fish sees light coming from a particular direction and interprets the angler to be in that direction. For example, if a 6-foot angler was 6 feet from the edge of the stream and the angle of incidence was 45 degrees, our angler would have stretched to approximately 9½ feet in the fish's eyes. Unfortunately, our trout spent very little time living in schools and was not exposed to the physics of refraction while in school. Why this preoccupation about where the fish sees you? Since most predators of large stream-dwelling fish are avian, any movement above the water triggers an instinctive

THE SCIENCE OF FLY-FISHING

FIG. 31. Relative refraction of light rays from angler

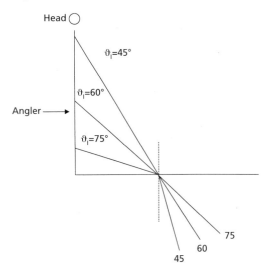

Head ◯

$\vartheta_I=45°$

$\vartheta_I=60°$

Angler ⟶

$\vartheta_I=75°$

75

60

45

fear in the fish. It is an advantage to any angler to keep a low profile to minimize detection by the fish and not send that prize fish scurrying for cover. The problem of detection is compounded by the fact that our unknowing angler is often flailing about a long fly rod that increases visual distortion. This may necessitate learning to cast in the horizontal plane in addition to maintaining that low profile.

Visual distortion due to refraction causes not only a displacement of the image relative to the object but a change in clarity of the above-water field of vision of the trout. The physics of refraction requires light rays from the lower part on an object to be bent more than those from the upper part. Note from the light ray diagram in figure 31 that, from the perspective of the fish, the lower part of the object is compressed or flattened more than the upper part (look at the spacing between the light rays). The lower part of the object, let's say below the angler's waist, is then fuzzy and out of focus to the fish compared to the top part, above the waist. If you crouch down at this same distance from the fish, then at this low angle your whole profile will appear distorted to the trout. Simply, the trout is probably not sure exactly what it is seeing. How low can one go? As we have discussed above, most of the light that strikes the water surface will be reflected at very low light angles. If the incident light ray is only 5 degrees or less above the horizon, no light will enter the water column, and in turn the fish cannot see objects below this angle. I'll do the math for you, so let's look at an example. To be totally invisible to the fish at the 5-degree angle, an angler 10 feet from the edge of the line of sight of the fish would have to crouch down to a height of 0.9 feet.

All the light rays that enter the water medium are refracted to a certain degree, some more than others. The result is that all the light from horizon to horizon is refracted into the shape of a cone with an apex angle of 97 degrees (fig. 32). The base of the cone, often referred to as Snell's window, is the width of the surface field of vision of the fish and depends upon the depth of the fish. The diameter of window is slightly more than twice as wide as the fish is deep. A trout at a depth of 8 inches would have a window of only 18 inches wide, and one at 2 feet a window of 4½ feet. In the former situation, the fish will only be able to visually detect prey or your fly a distance of 9 inches to either the left or right of its head. These small windows near the surface do pose a disadvantage to the fish, since it would not be able to detect prey outside the window. Outside the window, there is no refracted light from the surface, and the fish can't see out. On the plus side, as a fish is rising from deeper water to snatch a floating food item, the

FIG. 32. Schematic diagram of Snell's window

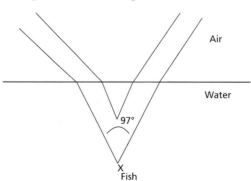

THE SCIENCE OF FLY-FISHING

fish can lock in on the prey as a result of the decreasing window's size. Mature trout are efficient predators and seldom miss their prey.

Since light rays in the center of the window aren't refracted at all, light passes straight through the water to the fish's eye. Without the visual distortion that results from refraction, objects in the middle of the fish's window will appear normal in size. Light rays near the edge of the window are bent and compressed the most, so visual distortion is most acute in this region. Objects near the outer limits of the fish's window are hard to discern with any clarity. An approaching angler will initially appear as an out-of-focus, compressed object. As the angler moves closer to the center of the window, the distortion decreases, and the trout will clearly see you. It is imperative, therefore, that you maintain that low profile.

The field of vision of trout to the outside environment also depends upon the nature of the water surface. In a pool with a fairly placid surface, the fish has a relatively good window on the outside world. In riffled water, the broken surface of the water makes it difficult for the fish to have a clear view of objects above the water surface. It's analogous to trying to look through a badly crumpled piece of cellophane. However, there is a tradeoff in that avian predators have difficulty in detecting fish through this turbulent, opaque water. Though riffled stretches of water are relatively shallow, fish feel moderately secure because of this visual isolation.

In very clear waters, wary trout may become leader "shy"; that is, the high transparency of the water allows the fish to easily see the fly-leader connection, and this may spook the trout, since leaders aren't part of its natural setting. In these cases, savvy anglers may switch from a monofilament to a fluorocarbon leader. Invented in the late 1940s in Japan for catching very finicky little fish, fluorocarbon has approximately the same index of refraction as water, so it is nearly invisible in the water.

Now that we have viewed refraction from the fish's perspective, how does refraction affect the fly angler pursuing that trophy fish? Consider the following scenario. A 17-inch brown trout is carefully searching the current flow for a morsel of food. Our angler, positioned a few feet upstream of the trout and poised to make a cast, sees this deep-holding trout. If the angler wants to place the fly just in front of the "nose" of the fish, will success be achieved? Light refracts away from the normal as it travels from the fish to the eyes of the angler. Due to this bending of the path of the light, the fish appears to be in a location where it isn't—a visual distortion. The image of the fish, what the angler sees, is displaced behind the actual holding place of the fish (fig. 33). The deeper the fish is holding, the greater will be the horizontal displacement. If the angler casts the fly to the image position, there is almost no chance of success, since the fly has landed behind the fish—an unnatural presentation. The effect of light refraction will also depress (top to bottom) the image of the fish, making it appear to be more elongated. This distortion can be frustrating to the angler who is attempting to see fish below the surface. Other objects like sticks, twigs, and weeds, being long and thin, may initially confuse the angler as to exactly what is being seen below the water surface.

FIG. 33. Displacement of image relative to object due to refraction from the perspective of the angler

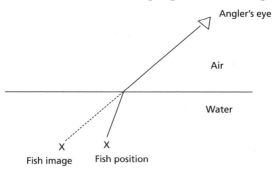

Angler's eye

Air

Water

X   X
Fish image   Fish position

Another maddening optical phenomenon to the angler is total internal reflection—the reflection of all incident light at the boundary between air and water. To understand total internal reflection, let's begin with a simple thought experiment. Suppose we submerge a light source below the water and point its beam upward toward the water-air boundary. Then suppose that the angle at which the beam intersects the water surface is altered (fig. 34). Based upon the optical properties of both water and air, we would expect both reflection and refraction. But that is not all we would observe. As the angle of incidence increases from 0 degrees to greater angles, the refracted ray becomes dimmer (there is less refraction); the reflected ray becomes brighter (there is more reflection); the angle of refraction approaches 90 degrees, and a refracted ray can no longer be seen. So in the case of our light beam in the water, there is some critical angle of incidence, which results in an angle of refraction of 90 degrees. For an incidence angle greater than the critical angle, all the light is reflected internally.

FIG. 34. Refraction and internal reflection of light

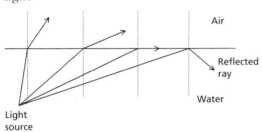

What does this simple experiment mean to our fly angler standing along the stream bank? The closer the angler is to the subsurface fish, the brighter and more visible the fish will be, since a greater portion of the light is refracted to the eyes of the angler than is reflected back into the water. As the angler backs away from the stream bank, the intensity of the refracted light decreases, and the fish does not appear as bright. Finally, at a particular distance from the fish, the fish is not at all visible to the angler, since no refracted light is reaching the angler's eyes.

As we have seen, many fish will orient themselves in the direction of the current flow. The anatomy of fish, with its eyes on both sides of its head, allows it to detect both prey and predator alike through a large arc. Trout have a field of vision of 330 degrees around themselves as compared to 176 degrees for humans. Though having a large zone of peripheral vision, the area of binocular vision is only 30 degrees. The depth perception provided by the binocular vision allows trout to judge the distance and speed of current-swept prey. Though a trout may see a potential prey in the "corner" of its eye, it often will not move any appreciable distance to have a closer look. Instead the fish focuses on a particular current seam or feeding channel. In areas of moderate current flow, the width of the channel is comparable to the zone of the fish's binocular vision. With increasing current speed, the angular width of the channel decreases, since the potential food items are moving rapidly past the trout's field of vision. The angler has a relatively narrow corridor to work with in the proper presentation of the fly. In still waters where the fish does not have to contend with currents, the visual scope of the fish increases, and the chances of success of the angler's offering also rise.

As we have just seen, the aquatic world of the fish is unique with regard to its optical properties. Though the specifics of these properties may seem daunting, understanding the basic properties of light and how fish visually perceive their environment will allow any angler to adjust his techniques to the ever-changing visual panorama of our water world.

TEN

Salmonids: Their History, Life Cycle, and Characteristics

PROBABLY NO OTHER FISHES HAVE BEEN PURSUED
so intently by fly anglers as trout, salmon, and their related
cousins. The literature abounds with tales of anglers fishing
small spring creeks for rainbow trout, venturing to the mountain streams of New Zealand to cast a fly at brown trout, and
angling the cold rivers of Iceland for Atlantic salmon. One
would be hard-pressed to pick up a fly-fishing magazine without finding such articles as "Ten Hot Spots for Trout in
Wyoming" or "How to Master the Two-Handed Spey Cast for
Salmon." This intense interest with these species has been documented well back into antiquity. Detailed drawings of trout
and salmon that date back ten thousand years before the birth
of Christ have been found in the caves of France and Spain.
During Caesar's occupation of Europe, the salmon was viewed
as a creature of considerable esteem. Romans were probably
the first to practice aquatic conservation measures—stocking
the rivers of their realm to replenish depleted reserves. When
the Romans left Britain in 410 BC, Anglo-Saxon invaders
brought with them some of the terms by which salmon is
known today—parr, smolt, and grisle. With the rise of the
feudal system, salmon became the prerogative of the nobility
and clergy and was ultimately proclaimed a "regal fish."

I will continue this historical vein by focusing on the
salmonids—trout, salmon, char, and other members of the
family Salmonidae. The term *family* is part of a taxonomic
classification scheme developed in the eighteenth century by
Carolus Linnaeus to arrange the biota into broad groupings
that share common traits. Proceeding from the most general

to the most specific, the following categories arise: Kingdom, Phylum, Class, Order, Family, Genus, and Species. All animals are denoted by two words—a name for the genus and a name for the species. The interested angler is encouraged to pursue the life history of her own favorite fish, whether it is a freshwater or saltwater species. It is simply beyond the scope of this chapter and the overall focus of the manuscript even to outline the biology of other fish.

Though the members of the Salmonidae family differ greatly in outward appearance, they are grouped together because they all have features in common—soft (no spines) fin rays, fine cycloid scales, and an adipose fin. The adipose fin is a relatively small appendage located between the dorsal and caudal fin, and its specific function is unclear to fisheries biologists.

Paleontological evidence places the early ancestors of trout and salmon back more than 35 million years ago—during the Oligocene epoch. As the Oligocene drew to a close, the salmon-like group divided into the genus of *Salmo* and *Oncorhynchus.* During the Pliocene epoch (1.5 to 5 million years ago), the former genus branched into the brown trout; and during the Miocene epoch (5 to 24 million years ago), the latter genus divided into the Pacific salmon species—pink, king, coho, chinook, and sockeye. In 1989, steelhead (sea-run rainbows) trout and cutthroat trout were included into the genus. On the other side of the salmonids tree, the genus *Salvelinus* divided into two branches during the Pliocene. One path included the bull trout, Dolly Varden, and char, while another path led to the brook and lake trout. In the late 1880s, R. W. Shufeldt concluded that the modern-day Salmonidae family had its origin about 2 million years ago.

Over time, variations in particular salmonids can occur as a result of genetic and environmental influences. These effects result in different biological strains within the species that exhibit a common ancestry with similar morphological characteristics but are physiologically distinct. That is, the organisms look the same, but their vital life processes are different. The unique geological, chemical, and biological characteristics of a particular watershed may lead to a brown trout that would physically appear the same, *phenotypically,* as a brown trout in a neighboring watershed with a different set of environmental characteristics. But the two fish would have a different genetic makeup, *genotypically,* and are considered to be different strains. The ice ages, a series of glacial advances and retreats over the last million years, have probably had the greatest impact on the development of new strains or species within the salmonids. George Power (1969) has argued that the barriers of ice and temperature played a key role in the evolution of freshwater varieties of salmon in eastern North America. And Anthony Netboy (1974) has postulated that the creation of the Alaska-Siberia land bridge resulted in the separation of what are now two distinct stocks of salmon—the Atlantic and Pacific. Occurring a mere twenty thousand years ago, which is a blip in geological time, the Wisconsin Ice Sheet had a profound impact on the salmonids. At that time, ice, thousands of feet thick, extended as far south as New York City and resulted in a geographical shift of fish populations. Many of the species, such as lake trout, char, and brook trout, that are presently found in the cooler climates of northern United States and Canada were common to regions much farther to the south. In contrast, those unlucky species that couldn't find water routes to the south became trapped in isolated watersheds and succumbed over time to the extreme cold.

Water temperature is probably the chief factor that determined the geographical distribution of these species. The reasons for this thermal dependence are varied: the evolutionary lineage of the species, the temperature dependence of a species's prey, and its innate instinct to reproduce. Aquatic organisms that can tolerate large ranges in temperature are referred to as *eurythermal.* If a species occupies a narrow temperature range, it is *stenothermal.* Most salmonids fall within the group of stenothermal organisms. For example, the optimal temperature range for brown trout is between 39°F and 68°F. The lower limit for survival is 32°F, and the upper limit is approximately 77°F. This narrow temperature tolerance has confined the North American brown trout to the temperate latitudes and a habitat generally associated with high topographical features. Salmonids are generally absent from warmwater streams because of their "genetic programming" that simply does not allow them to survive at relatively high temperatures. In addition, most fish, including the salmonids, are "cold-blooded," or poikilothermic, having an internal body temperature similar to that of their environment. In general, the warmer the water of a poikilotherm, within its tolerance range, the greater its metabolic rate. This is the speed at which energy-releasing reactions (conversion of food to energy) occur within an organism. Research has shown that the growth rate of brown trout increased with temperature from 42°F to between 54°F and 59°F, but there was a marked decline in growth at 35°F. Thus brown trout can generally not meet their energy demands at temperatures above 68°F. Growth rates generally decline in most species when they reach their upper thermal limit, but for cold stenothermal species, like salmonids, it is more pronounced.

R. W. Dunfield (1985) postulates that the evolution of a species is reflected in the life cycle of the individual in that species. For example, he states that many scientists believe the salmon was originally a freshwater-dwelling organism but was forced into the marine environment by the advance of the ice sheets. That is, the salmon had to change and adapt in order to survive. It can be argued then that an understanding of the life cycle of an organism gives us a glimpse into its evolutionary history.

The life cycle of an animal consists of distinctive stages of growth and maturity from its conception ultimately to its death. Within each stage of the life cycle, the animal will perform specific functions in specific locales. The composite of these actions is called the life history of the animal.

The life cycle of salmonids consist of four distinct stages:
1. Spawning—This time frame includes migration to the spawning ground, construction of the nest on the bottom, and deposition of the eggs;
2. Incubation—The period of time spanning from the laying of the eggs to the emergence of the hatched fry into water;

3. Juvenile—This is a period of growth from fry to adult;
4. Adult—During this stage, the fish is sexually mature, capable of reproducing, and attains its maximum size.

The duration for each of these stages will vary among the salmonids and is also dependent upon environmental factors.

With regard to spawning and egg incubation, all salmonids seek similar types of niches and have similar nesting strategies. They prefer to build a nest, or *redd,* on a gravel-bottomed stream. The initial stage in redd-building involves the female creating a depression in the substrate by using her broad caudal fin to sweep out finer sediments and pebbles. The female lying flat on the streambed and jerking her tail upward, thereby pulling the particles into the current, accomplishes this. The digging continues until the larger substrate particles are reached, and a depression *(pitt)* is formed. These particles will form the bed for the female's deposition of the eggs and fertilization of eggs by the male. After depositing her eggs, the female moves upstream of the first depression to begin anew the digging process. Not only is another depression created for another round of egg-laying but also the excavated gravel that is carried downstream will cover the initial egg deposits. In each receptacle the eggs are surrounded by gravel particles decreasing in size from that found on the floor of the depression to those on top of the eggs (fig. 35).

Trout and salmon are less prolific than most other fish with regard to the number of eggs deposited. Research has shown that a 10-pound rainbow trout (a big fish by anyone's standard) deposits only about 4,000 eggs, compared to 200,000 eggs for a walleye of the same size. Salmonid eggs incubate from 1 to 5 months, depending upon the species. The

FIG. 35. Cross-section of a salmonid's redd in a stream

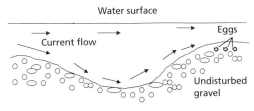

incubating eggs require a consistent flow of water through the gravel to deliver oxygen to the eggs and remove waste products. This long incubation period subjects the eggs to many hazards, including diseases and floods. In addition, if the eggs are not sufficiently covered by the gravel particles, they will be quickly eaten by a host of predators, such as crayfish, insects, and fish.

After hatching, the fry exhibit very little mobility and continue to live in the gravel for a period of time. They do not actively feed at this stage but obtain their nourishment from the attached yolk sac. After several weeks, they gain enough strength to wiggle through the gravel and begin their free-swimming stage.

Once the fry emerge from the redd, the life cycle processes that characterized all salmonids during the spawning and incubation periods end. Depending upon the particular species, the life histories of the juveniles and adults can be markedly different. Though all salmonid fry emerge from their eggs into freshwater and all sexually mature adults spawn in freshwater, the intervening period can be marked by considerable migration from their natal streams for some species and relatively little movement by other species. Table 7 summarizes the major life history strategies that characterize the salmonids. It may be confusing to see trout falling within various categories. But the evolutionary process has allowed for development of various strains of trout that employ different survival strategies. Though most strains of brook, rainbow, brown, and cutthroat trout are stream-dwelling, there are strains of these species that migrate to salt water—sea run trout. Let's take a closer look at the life histories and cycles of selected salmonids.

BROOK TROUT *(Salvelinus fontinalis)*. Maybe to the surprise of some, brook trout are not really trout but are members of the char genus. Genetically and morphologically speaking, it is close to a trout, but there are marked distinctions between the species. Nick Karas develops the unique lineage of this species in his in-depth study *Brook Trout* (1997): "*Salvelinus* is an old Germanic word for Arctic char found in the Alps. The literature just says that it's an old name; no one

TABLE 7. Migratory strategies of recently spawned salmonids

Strategy	Time Period	Species
Migration to ocean	Immediately after emerging	Pink and chum salmon
Migration to lake	Immediately after emerging	Kokanee salmon
Migration to ocean	1 to 3 years in stream	Coho and chinook salmon, trout
Migration to lake	1 to 3 years in stream	Trout
Stream-dwelling	Entire lifetime	Trout

has ever explained what it means. *Fontinalis* is easy: It's Latin (*fons*) and means 'dweller near spring,' which is just what brookies do. *Charr* . . . is an adequate name for brook trout. It's derived from the Celtic word *cear,* which mean 'blood.' The name is appropriate because the sides of all charrs—the only charr they saw in Europe was the Arctic charr—turn blood red during the fall spawning period." Spawning male brook trout undergo a dramatic color change, an intense orange-red coloration on the underside.

The first European settlers in America were very familiar with the brown trout of their native rivers. But it made no difference to this hardy band of Pilgrims that the fish they observed in their newly named streams were really char. They looked like trout and were found in brooks, thus brook trout.

The origins of brook trout can be traced back to eastern North America. There is no evidence of this species west of the Mississippi. The current distribution of brook trout encompasses most of the eastern Canadian provinces, including the Canadian Maritimes, Labrador, and Newfoundland. This northward extent can be attributed to, in part, the fact that brook trout require colder water temperatures than either rainbow or brown trout. In the United States, the brook trout's range covers all of New England and New York. It extends southward through most of Pennsylvania, then straddles the Appalachian range to northern Georgia. Because of its eastern heritage the brook trout is often referred to as "native" trout in some eastern states.

Brook trout spawn in the fall, with peak months being October and November. But in their high-latitude habitats, they may spawn as early as September. The urge to spawn appears to be triggered primarily by the decreasing hours of daylight during the fall. While they may have spent the summer in large rivers or lakes because of their abundant food supply, they will migrate to smaller streams that have a supply of cold, well-aerated water flowing over a gravel bottom. Compared to other trout species, brook trout build their redds in the stream near or on top of up-welling springs that allow for a flow of oxygenated water through the incubating eggs. Brook trout can also spawn in lakes that have these springs originating out of the bottom. An average-sized female of about 6 inches can deposit approximately 100 eggs in the redd. The incubation period of the eggs is a function of water temperature. Colder water environments have a longer period than warmer water streams. On the average, the eggs hatch two to three months after they are spawned.

The hatched fry will remain within the protective cover of the redd for another month or two. Once they attain the free-swimming stage of about 2 inches in length, they abandon the redd in search of food and new forms of protection. Growth rates and size are strongly influenced by the environment. The life span of this species is on the order of four years, during which they attain an average size of 9 to 12 inches. But record-setting brook trout have been measured at over 20 inches in length and upward of 9 pounds.

Brook trout are "opportunistic" feeders, feeding on whatever is available. This nonselective feeding behavior is necessary for their survival in some of the relatively barren freestone mountain streams they inhabit. Smaller fish, in the 4- to 8-inch range, feed primarily on aquatic and terrestrial insects. Larger fish, 8 to 12 inches, will feed on minnows and salamanders. Brook trout are diurnal feeders, feeding as long as there is sufficient light. But the knowledgeable angler also recognizes the preferred feeding patterns of brook trout—feeding best in early morning and late afternoon periods timed to insect hatches. With increasing water temperature common during midday or summer, brook trout may be reluctant to feed, and the angler is hard-pressed to entice them to the fly.

RAINBOW TROUT *(Oncorhynchus mykiss)*. Rainbow trout occur as both freshwater residents and sea-run populations. The sea-run populations, called steelheads, are found predominantly in the Pacific Northwest. Closely related species to the rainbow include the golden trout *(O. aguabonita)* and the cutthroat trout *(O. clarki)*.

From its overall silvery appearance, the rainbow's color varies depending upon its habitat, age, sex, and degree of maturity. In general, most have a dark back, silvery belly, and a prominent lateral pink/red line (the characteristic from which it derives its name) extending from behind the gill cover to the tail. Small black spots are found above the lateral line, covering the back and fins.

These trout are native to the Pacific Coast of the United States, extending from Alaska to northern Mexico and eastward to the western slopes of the Rocky Mountains. This species has been introduced throughout the United States and to many countries in both the northern and southern hemispheres. These transplanted rainbow trout have displaced brook trout over much of its historic range in the southeastern United States. The remaining high-altitude brook trout habitat is generally unsuitable for the rainbow.

Most rainbow trout populations spawn in the spring, laying their eggs in March. Spawning occurs in stream gravel beds similar to that used by the brook trout. But their reproductive potential is significantly higher than that of the brook trout, with the average-sized female depositing between 800 and 1,000 eggs. The period of incubation is short in comparison to either the brook or brown trout, with the fry emerging from the redd in May.

The diet of rainbows is similar to that of brook trout—invertebrates. But the larger rainbows often show a greater preference for small fish than do brook trout. From an angler's perspective, rainbow trout may be marginally more difficult to catch than brook trout because they are more selective in their choice of food items. Even during the best of times, rainbow trout can be downright fussy about what and when they eat. On the flip side, rainbows have the potential to attain a much larger size (12 to 18 inches) than brook trout, particularly those rainbows that occupy the more fertile spring creeks and large lakes.

Among fly anglers the fighting ability of a hooked rainbow is legendary. Research has shown that a moderately sized rainbow can accelerate from standstill to about 20 miles per hour in one second. From the moment it feels the sting of the hook, it is moving at more than 30 feet per second, enough to make your fly reel "sing" from the line that is rapidly leaving it. These trout will also put on quite an aerial display as they try to throw the hook. Capable of jumping numerous times during the course of the fight, a rainbow trout can easily jump three or four times its body length.

BROWN TROUT *(Salmo trutta)*. This species has the distinction of being the first trout to be described in Linneaus's 1758 edition of *The System of Nature.* The name of this trout is derived from its coloration—the dorsal area is usually brown. It resembles its relative, the Atlantic salmon *(Salmo salar).* Both have black spots extending from their upper back to approximately their lateral line. Though both species may occur in the same area, freshwater brown trout can be distinguished from Atlantic salmon because of the greater density of body spotting.

Brown trout are native only to Europe and Asia. The natural distribution of brown trout ranges from the waters of northern Norway and Russia southward to the Atlas Mountains of North Africa. On their western limit, brown trout are indigenous to Iceland and extend eastward to Afghanistan. As with other trout species, they have been widely introduced to other parts of the globe. They made their first appearance in eastern North America at the end of the nineteenth century with shipments from Germany in 1883 and from Loch Leven, Scotland, in 1885. Today the range of this species is found throughout the United States wherever there is suitable habitat.

Though having similar nesting strategies to that of rainbow and brook trout, brown trout spawn later than brook trout, generally in the months of November and December. The falling water temperatures and the decreasing amount of daylight trigger the spawning. Females of this species are quite fertile, having higher reproductive potential that either rainbow or brook trout. The eggs incubate in the gravel over winter. Keyed to water temperature, the eggs hatch in late February and March. The fry remain in the gravel for another three to six weeks until their yolk sac is fully absorbed. Although anadromous strains occur, brown trout usually reside in their natal streams. As the trout matures, it may migrate downstream to wider and deeper stream channels.

Ralph Behnke, a fisheries biologist at Colorado State University, has determined that the life history of this species is strongly influenced by its environment. In small streams, they feed mainly on aquatic insects and rarely grow to a weight of more than 2 to 3 pounds during a life span of three to four years. In larger rivers and lakes, where small fish are a plentiful food source, brown trout may easily reach weights of over 20 pounds during a ten- to fifteen-year life expectancy. The all-tackle International Game Fish Association record is over 40 pounds.

Many knowledgeable anglers will argue that the brown trout is the most difficult of the trout species to catch on a fly. Since some anglers are prone to hyperbole, is there any truth to this perception, or is it just another fish tale? Most of the data, such as catch per effort, catch per stretch of stream, or portion of browns in total fish sample, unequivocally point to the conclusion that brown trout are indeed more difficult to catch than the other species. For example, data collected from the North Platte River in Wyoming showed that the ratio of brown to rainbow trout residing in the rivers was 78:22. But the catch ratio of these two species was 35:65. In other words, brown trout make up 78 percent of the total number of fish in the river in comparison to only 22 percent for rainbow trout. Yet, only 35 percent of the total fish caught were browns, and 65 percent were rainbows. Theories attempting to explain this result have centered on the proclivity of browns for dense cover and their nocturnal feeding habits, which eliminate some angling pressure. At this stage, the angling jury is still out.

ATLANTIC SALMON *(Salmo salar)*. This is the only species of salmon found within the Atlantic as contrasted to the five Pacific species. It may appear odd to the reader that it is classified taxonomically as a member of the "trout" genus *Salmo,* rather than the Pacific salmon genus *Oncorhynchus.* The name *salmon* originated in Europe and initially applied to the Atlantic salmon in European waters. The name came to the New World with the early settlers, where it carried over to the Atlantic salmon on this side of the ocean. Because of their prodigious jumping ability, American salmon were often called the "leaping fish." This title eventually resulted in its scientific name, *Salmo salar*—salmon the leaper. There has been some effort by taxonomic "purists" to change the name of the Atlantic salmon to make it fit with its taxonomic lineage of the trout, but these ventures have been unsuccessful because of the historical roots of the name and the prevalent place of the name *Atlantic salmon* in the literature.

The historic range of this species is the northern Atlantic and its freshwater tributaries from Quebec to Connecticut in North America stretching to Iceland, and from the Arctic Circle to Portugal in Europe. The Atlantic salmon is an anadromous fish; that is, depending upon coastal rivers to spawn. From a genetic standpoint, it appears that Atlantic salmon are very river specific in their attributes, specifically designed for particular river systems. Their mating within the river system of their birth, with only a very small number wandering to other rivers, has reenforced this genetic programming. Unfortunately, many of these historic freshwater runs have deteriorated or been eliminated as suitable habitat for the salmon.

Salmon return to their natal rivers in North America anytime between May and October. While some early arrivers may linger in pools for a period of time and others travel directly to their nesting sites, all will spawn in the fall. During the spawning runs, salmon do not need to feed, so they do not have to take a fly. But to the joy of all salmon anglers, they will instinctively strike out at mainly wet flies, depending upon such variables as water and light levels. The patient fly angler can trigger the salmon's feeding reflex with the proper presentation of the fly.

Studies have shown that the number of eggs deposited is a function of the female's size. Females produce an average of about 800 eggs per pound of body weight. A 10-pound salmon is capable of depositing up to 8,000 eggs during the spawning season. Though laws protect salmon from any angling pressure while they are on the spawning beds, most anglers respect the procreation ritual of this magnificent animal. During spawning, the Atlantic salmon turns a much darker color, often bronze or dark brown—looking remarkably like its close relative, the brown trout. Unlike the species of Pacific salmon, the Atlantic salmon does not expire after spawning. Those that have survived the spawning process are called *kelts*. A proportion of this population will return to the sea during the fall. But another segment will winter over in the river, only to return to the sea the following spring. Those that descend to the ocean during this period are emaciated, having lost between 25 and 35 percent of their body weight. The rigors of spawning and migration, coupled with salmon's propensity not to feed in fresh water, have taken their toll. These skinny spring salmon are called *racers* by those fortunate anglers who have caught these fish. The next spawning cycle for the survivors will be from twelve to fifteen months after the initial spawn. Some Atlantic salmon have repeated the reproductive cycle three to four times during their life span of eight to ten years.

The eggs incubate over the winter, and thousands of tiny salmon alevins (sac fry) emerge during the early spring. These alevins receive nourishment from an attached yolk sac and find protection within the gravel streambed. In about six weeks the yolk sac is absorbed, and the fry emerge from the gravel to feed in the river. After these fry have attained a length of about three inches, they are called *parr*. Their eight to eleven dark vertical bars on their sides easily identify salmon parr. These young salmon remain within the protective confines of the river from two to six years. The nursery-like environment provided by the river must both satisfy the nutritional needs of the growing salmon and provide suitable cover from predators.

As the time approaches for the salmon to enter the salty realm, the parr undergoes significant morphological and physiological changes. The parr bands disappear to be replaced by a silvery appearance, better suited for camouflage in its new environment. Osmoregulatory processes occur within the fish, necessary for its survival in the salt water. These smolts are now ready to migrate downstream during May and June to enter the ocean. The period that salmon spend in the ocean varies from as little as one year to three years. Salmon spending only one winter in the marine environment are called *grisle.* While a grisle that has spent only one year at sea may weigh from three to six pounds, salmon that fattened up on herring and capelin may weigh up to thirty pounds.

Though its value as a sport fish is not exaggerated, being a hard fighter and strong jumper, some anglers feel that salmon lack the cunning to be a truly worthy adversary. Though anglers may have the tendency to overly assign human values, like intelligence levels, to fish, evidence points to the fact that these fish can be readily caught when they are in the mood. Clumsy approaches and imperfect casts, though seeming to violate the rules of fly-fishing success, have not deterred the salmon from striking the fly.

PACIFIC SALMON. These salmon are all members of the genus *Oncorhynchus* that include pink, sockeye, chum, chinook, and coho salmon. Each species of salmon has several runs or home territories to which it returns at a specific time of the year. Biologists usually refer to wild salmon stocks by their run (time of return) and race (river of origin)—for example, Snake River spring chinook or Sacramento River winter chinook. But a chinook salmon from one river may be quite different genetically from chinook of another river. This vast genetic diversity has allowed salmon to survive for two million years as they stake a claim to a particular stream or adapt to a changing watershed.

Though their spawning strategies and life cycle are similar to that of Atlantic salmon, a major difference is that Pacific salmon spawn only once in their lifetime. Pacific salmon die soon after spawning; their corpses become food for higher-level carnivores (bears, eagles) or a source of nutrients to the environment as a result of decomposition.

Each species of Pacific salmon pursues a slightly different life history strategy that can confer advantages and disadvantages, depending on the environmental pressures that a given stock may encounter. Both chum *(O. keta)* and pink *(O. gorbuscha)* migrate seaward almost immediately (hours to days) upon emergence from the redd in the spring. While dependent upon adequate discharge and suitable water quality during the spawning and incubation periods, droughts or poor water quality during the summer can be less of a problem to these species. After spending from one and a half (pink) to three (chum) years at sea, they ultimately reach their spawning grounds as late as November and December. The male of the species undergoes major morphological changes during the spawning period. Since spawning males often develop large canine-like teeth, chum salmon are often referred to as *dog salmon.* Spawning males of the pink salmon species develop a pronounced hump of their back and are called *humpies.*

At the other end of the rearing spectrum, the fry of the sockeye *(O. nerka)* and coho *(O. kisutch)* salmon may remain in fresh water from one to two years. Falling in the middle of the pack are chinook *(O. tshawytscha)* stocks that can vary considerably in the length of time (one month to one year) required for freshwater rearing of the fry. This built-in flexibility limits the impact of flow or environmental perturbations on this species.

Of the five species, coho salmon tend to be the most widely distributed with regard to spawning habitats, ranging from large rivers to small creeks. In the latter habitat, coho salmon can be negatively impacted because these small channels are susceptible to anthropogenic and natural perturbations. In contrast, sockeye and chinook salmon tend to be more clustered and selective than coho as they go about their reproductive business. For example, sockeye salmon often select specific aquatic environments that are part of a larger lake complex. In a single lake system, there can be different stocks, each uniquely suited to spawning in an outlet river, inlet river, or along the lakeshore. Chinook salmon are fond of stream reaches that offer stable discharges, such as segments that are recharged from above by a lake. Since pink and chum salmon are less capable of surmounting obstacles—in particular, chum salmon are not good leapers—they use the lower reaches of stream systems for their spawning nests.

While at sea, all of these salmon exhibit a silvery coloration with spotting on the back, upper head, and fins. During the spawning period, each species, particularly the males, undergoes distinctive color changes—ranging from olive-brown for chinook salmon to a totally red body for sockeye salmon. One of the most radical changes found in the spawning males of all Pacific salmon, except the chum, is the development of a kype, where the jaw becomes extended and hooked.

Since salmon may cease feeding once they enter the river, many West-Coast anglers target these species at the mouth of the river or in the near-shore environment. Chinook and coho top the sporting list of many fly anglers. Also called king salmon, chinooks are truly the kings of the angling community due to their large size (over 100 pounds) and fighting nature when hooked. While chinook will put on a determined subsurface struggle, the smaller (20–30 pounds) coho salmon will take its battle to the surface in a flashy aerial display. Though it is the smallest of the salmon—usual size is 3 to 5 pounds—fly anglers should not overlook pink salmon because of their spunky nature. During their summer migration along the coastal shoreline of their natal rivers, fly anglers target them as they congregate in large schools. In comparison, the last two species, chum and sockeye salmon, are not highly sought by most saltwater fly anglers, who often cite their lack of size and/or fighting ability. In addition, sockeye salmon are plankton feeders, filtering these tiny organisms from the water with their gill rakers. This feeding behavior makes them quite difficult to catch on hook and line.

But fly anglers are often a contentious bunch. Tell them this technique won't work and they will try their darnedest to disprove you. For every angler who expresses a negative view with regard to Pacific salmon taking a fly in fresh water, others vehemently argue that Pacific salmon, like their Atlantic cousins, will strike a fly during their river journey to the spawning grounds. Let's establish some common ground. Alaskan fishing lodges that can charge their clients hundreds of dollars a day to fish for river salmon wouldn't be in business unless their anglers caught freshwater salmon on a fly.

The main key to fly-fishing success for river salmon is to know thine enemy! Each species has its own idiosyncrasies, habits, favorite holding places, and preferred feeding strategies that need to be recognized by the angler. These differences may even vary within the same species as we consider various strains that occupy different river systems. One of the starting places to begin understanding our foe is its life history. For example, the long freshwater residency of coho and chinook salmon have "programmed" them to actively strike at a fly. It is argued that this response is the result of the time spent in the fresh water devouring natural prey. In contrast, chum and pink salmon have not been predisposed to take a fly because of their short freshwater residency. In addition, some salmon, such as the chum, become aggressive at they approach sexual maturity; others like the coho and chinook assume a more laid-back posture. If the behavior of salmon is conditioned by both their freshwater and marine experiences, then the angler needs to take this into consideration in even the most fundamental of fly-fishing tasks—the presentation of the fly. Coho salmon, having spent a minimum of at least a year in both fresh water and salt water, have a propensity to chase prey. A lively presentation of the fly, such as stripping line in, can lead to success. Chinook salmon will often position themselves along deep ledges, waiting for the current to supply their easy meal. A fly passively drifted in the current will often incite a take.

ARCTIC CHAR *(Salvelinus alpinus).* As its name implies, this species is found at high latitudes. It is the most northerly of all freshwater fish, native to the far northern streams and lakes of North America, Asia, Europe, Iceland, and Greenland.

The coloration of sea-run adults varies from blue-green on the back, shading to silver on the sides. Like all chars, members of the genus *Salvelinus,* the Arctic char has light-colored spots on its body. But it can be distinguished from it closest relatives, the salmon and trout, by the white coloration of its abdominal region and the lighter shading on the leading edge of its fins. Spawning fish change significantly in coloration, turning bright red on their sides, belly, and lower fins. Because of the variation in color associated with sea-run, landlocked, and spawning char, it is almost impossible for the casual observer to use appearance to distinguish the Arctic char from its closest relatives, the Dolly Varden *(Salvelinus malma)* and bull trout *(Salvelinus confluentus).* Even biologists have difficulty separating these species using only external characteristics and rely on more detailed laboratory analysis for positive identification. All three species require cold water (temperatures 39°F or less) for spawning; and spawning sites include main channels of coastal rivers (Dolly Varden), small inland tributaries (bull trout), and quiet pools (Arctic char).

Much to the joy of the growing number of anglers pursuing these fish, Arctic char are tailor-made for fly-fishing. Since it feeds as it migrates up the river to spawn, there is no debate on whether these fish will take a fly. Upon snatching a fly, the hooked fish will often make a strong run to the swifter water, where the struggle will continue. Char are just as likely to rise to a surface presentation as to a fly fished deep in the water column. When rising, these fish may be found throughout the stream reach except for the fast water in the main current channel. However, when the char are not visibly feeding on the surface, the angler can increase his chance by understanding some of the behavioral characteristics of this species. The junction of a lower-order stream emptying into a higher-order stream is always worth a few casts. Char may congregate here because some of these small creeks function as spawning grounds. They may gather in numbers at the confluence of these waters before heading upstream to spawn. In addition, the colder mountain water from these lower-order streams can provide ideal holding spots for char that are denied the cold, deep pockets of the main stream by salmon unwilling to share these sites.

In contrast, the bull trout and Dolly Varden are not highly rated as game fish. The Dolly Varden, in particular, has not won over the hearts of many anglers, since it has the unenviable reputation as a predator on the eggs and young of other trout and salmon. In the recent past, officials in Alaska have paid a bounty on all Dollies, resulting in the elimination of thousands of these fish. While the Dolly Varden is definitely guilty of eating these eggs, research has shown that most of these eggs have drifted from the redd and have little chance of hatching.

Though the salmonids have survived and adapted to changes in climates, watersheds, and stream reaches for over tens of thousands of years, the greatest threats to their continued survival are humans. In the relatively short span of human existence, this impact, primarily within the last century, has been profound and in some cases irreversible. The next chapter details some of the threats to the salmonids and possible solutions.

ELEVEN

Threats to the Survival of the Salmonids

YOU ARE PROBABLY READING THIS BOOK BECAUSE you have a passion for trout or salmon and a keen interest in the streams and lakes that you fly-fish. But over the last few decades, both species and habitat alike have been at the epicenter of significant change, heated debates, and a blurring-together of fact with fiction. This relentless increase in pressure on the salmonids has taken many forms—rampant development, habitat alteration, disease, waste products of an industrialized society, and even stresses from careless and unknowing anglers. With the growth in the popularity of fly-fishing in the United States must also come a new breed of educated and concerned anglers attuned to the threats that the salmonids face, without which there can be no quality fly-fishing.

One popular outgrowth of this movement toward a more knowledgeable angler is the practice of catch-and-release. Though many fly anglers would simply consider it unthinkable to kill a trout, one of the most frequently asked questions is whether the released fish actually survives. Though we can generally answer in the affirmative that many do indeed live to fight again, the survival rate depends upon the angler and a number of factors. Many anglers are simply not aware of the proper techniques in both fighting and handling a fish. What we do in these situations can mean the difference between a healthy fish strongly swimming away or one that struggles in the current, ultimately succumbing to the stress of the encounter. The thrill that a hooked fish provides to the angler can be quite intoxicating, as the fish may jump, make sustained runs, and hunker down in the current in its attempt to escape. But critical to the survival of the fish is how quickly the fish is fought and landed. Essentially, a short fight and a quick release increase the chances of survival of the fish. The degree of fight in a fish depends upon the nature and functioning of its muscles. What needs to be provided to the muscle for it to perform at a sustained level of activity? All muscles depend upon an energy source and oxygen. Both of these are transported to the muscles as a result of the circulatory system of the fish. But there are physiological limitations about how much energy and oxygen the heart and blood can transport to the muscles. As the fish struggles to regain its freedom, ultimately the oxygen in the muscles become depleted, the energy supply is exhausted, and metabolic wastes (lactic acid) accumulate in the muscles. Lactic acid is what makes our muscles sore after an intense period of physical exertion. If the fish is unable to eliminate this lactic acid buildup in a timely fashion, ultimately the fish succumbs to its weakened state. Research has shown that playing a fish for an extended period of time in warm water decreases its chance of survival. Because of the functional dependence of temperature on dissolved oxygen concentration, the fish is unable to satisfy its oxygen needs. In warm water the lactic acid accumulates quickly in the muscle tissue, and the fish tires much more rapidly. In addition, removing an exhausted fish from the water before releasing it further decreases its chance for survival. A Canadian study showed that rainbow trout exposed to the atmosphere for thirty seconds had a 27 percent mortality rate, and it increased to 72 percent for an exposure period of sixty seconds.

Once you have quickly played the fish, your next task is to revive the fish before releasing it. But what if this fish is that trophy rainbow trout or coho salmon you have been trying to catch for years and you want to determine its weight? Lifting it from the water, particularly by means of its gills, puts undue stress on the fish, and your hands may wipe off the protective mucous coating on the fish's surface. This slime helps prevent infection by waterborne disease. One solution is to keep the fish in the water and take some quick measurements of the dimensions of its body. Empirical research has shown that, depending upon the body shape of the fish, a particular combination of dimensional measurements can be used to estimate the weight of the fish. The formula for estimating the weight in pounds of most salmonids is length times girth times girth divided by 800. All measurements are in inches, and the girth is measured around the thickest portion of the fish. For example, a 17-inch rainbow trout with a girth of 9 inches has an estimated weight of 1.7 pounds. Though the result is essentially an educated guess about the weight, it beats telling those "whoppers"! To revive the fish, hold it gently under the belly and by the tail, making especially certain to keep it upright in the water. If you are fishing in a stream, hold the fish facing into the current to allow the oxygen-laden water to flow over its gills. In still water, you may have to move the fish back and forth in order to get the water flowing over its gills. When the fish recovers, let it swim from your hands.

That trout that you released back into the stream may still not be out of harm's way. One of the most insidious environmental problems that affect the salmonids is acid deposition—the falling of acids and acid-forming compounds from the atmosphere to the earth's surface. To fully understand the complex nature of this threat requires an introduction to the definition of an acid and its various natural and anthropogenic sources.

A measure of the acidity of a solution is expressed in terms of pH, where pH (potential of hydrogen) is a measure of the hydrogen ion (H^+) concentration in a solution. In symbolic form the pH is expressed as pH = $-\log [H^+]$. Based upon this relationship, chemists have developed the pH scale that is a measure of the relative acidity or alkalinity of a solution. The pH scale ranges from 0 to 14, with a value of 7 considered neutral. Values less than 7 are acidic and above 7 are alkaline. Table 8 depicts some typical solutions and their associated pH values. Note from the above relationship the logarithmic dependence of pH on the hydrogen ion concentration, which means that scale is logarithmic. What does this mean with regard to comparing different solutions? For each unit drop in

TABLE 8. pH scale

Value	Solution
0	Hydrochloric acid
1	Stomach acid
2	Lemon juice
3	Wine
4	Tomatoes
5	Black coffee
6	Milk
7	Pure water
8	Seawater
9	Baking soda
10	Milk of magnesia
11	Ammonia
12	Washing soda
13	Oven cleaner
14	Sodium hydroxide

pH the acidity increases tenfold. For example, a solution with a pH of 3 is 10 times more acidic than a solution with a pH of 4, and 100 times more acidic than a pH of 5.

While distilled water is neutral, it might be surprising to learn that precipitation is naturally somewhat acidic. The carbon dioxide gas that occurs naturally in the atmosphere dissolves in the precipitation to form a relatively weak (pH = 5.0 to 5.6) carbonic acid solution. Consequently, acid rain is then defined as having a pH below 5.0.

Acid rain has directly been linked to industrial and automobile emissions that have contributed airborne pollutant gases into the atmosphere. In particular, sulfur dioxide and nitrogen oxides react chemically with moisture and another compound (hydroxyl radical) in the presence of sunlight to form dilute drops of sulfuric and nitric acids. When the droplets of sulfuric and nitric acids dissolve in rain, the resultant precipitation can be quite acidic—hence, acid rain. Acidic rain is only one component of what is commonly referred to as wet deposition, which also includes acid fog and snow. Dry deposition occurs when particles of sulfate and nitrate salts fall on the ground. These particles may react with surface and ground water to form acidic solutions.

As these oxides react chemically in the atmosphere to form the acids, atmospheric circulation plays a key role in the subsequent transfer of these acids. Although some studies have shown that acid precipitation may be more than a regional phenomenon, areas immediately downwind of pollution sources are most susceptible to acidic effects. The industrialized Midwest, with its coal-fired plants, is thought to be a major source of sulfur dioxide. With predominantly westerly winds, the precipitation over the eastern sector of the United States has pH values ranging between 4.0 and 4.5.

Recall that precipitation is only one component of the hydrologic cycle that entails the movement of water through various reservoirs. The result is that numerous streams and lakes in the eastern United States have shown increasingly lower pH values over the past few decades. Researchers from Cornell University have documented that more than half of the 1,400 lakes and ponds in the Adirondacks are too acidic to support aquatic life. Studies conducted in the watersheds of the Appalachian Mountains showed significant increase in acidity in more than 70 percent of its streams—many of them prime trout waters.

Different watersheds are not equally affected by, or sensitive to, acid deposition. Some watersheds have the capability of buffering the pH; that is, to neutralize the acids that are added to the watershed. These watersheds maintain a relatively constant pH value that can support a wide spectrum of aquatic life. Factors that are important in controlling the pH include the composition of the underlying bedrock, nature of the soil, type of vegetative cover, microbial activity, and topographic features. The buffering capacity of the environment is determined by the amount of bicarbonate and carbonate ions present in the water. Soils and bedrock that are high in calcium carbonate (limestone) have the ability to neutralize the input of acids. The process is analogous to taking a commercial brand of an antacid to soothe indigestion resulting from the production of stomach acid.

The limestone streams of Pennsylvania, such as the Big Spring Creek, Le Tort Spring, and Falling Spring Branch, can and do receive relatively large acidic inputs, but pH levels in these streams remain relatively high and stable thanks to their high alkalinity. As a result, these streams have secured their place in fly-fishing lore because of the challenges they present to anglers and the healthy population of trout they support. In contrast, a number of streams draining the Appalachian Mountains in eastern West Virginia are not particularly inviting to trout because of the high level of acidity. The problem is the underlying shale bedrock that provides little buffering to the acidic rain and runoff. Similarly, in the Adirondack Mountains of New York state, the underlying bedrock of the watersheds contains little calcium carbonate; therefore, the lakes and streams of this region are very susceptible to acidification. In this region the rocks contain abundant silicate minerals that are not effective buffering agents. Studies have shown that the most acid-sensitive areas are associated with the mountainous terrain of the Appalachians and Adirondacks. The problem is compounded by the fact that in the higher elevations of this mountainous landscape most of the trees are conifers, which are intrinsically high in tannic acid. The decaying wood and root system of these conifers leach tannic acid into water, staining it brown. With enough time, brook trout have adapted to tannic acid waters, but other trout cannot tolerate these highly acidic waters and instead occupy stream reaches at lower elevations.

The acidic tolerance of aquatic life in streams and lakes is species dependent. The lower pH limit for rainbow trout is approximately 5.5, but brown and brook trout can tolerate a pH of 5.0 and 4.5, respectively. In other words, brook trout can inhabit waters that are ten times more acidic than comparable aquatic environments holding rainbow trout. Acidified waters that were once cohabitated by rainbows and brooks are now the sole preserve of brook trout. The aquatic food chain is also disrupted, since major food items such as mayflies can survive only with pH values above 5.5. To many biologists studying the effects of acid deposition on the environment, aquatic insects have become the proverbial "canary in the mineshaft"—the first to signal a decrease in water quality. A classic study of an acidified lake in Canada showed that a surprising number of changes occurred relatively rapidly in the lake. The minnow, *Pimephales promelas,* and the freshwater shrimp, *Mysis relicat,* disappeared at pH levels of 5.6 to 6.0. The alga, *Mougeotia,* began to proliferate and completely covered the lake bottom. Certain metals began to diffuse from the bottom sediments into the water. As the pH decreased to 5.0, more species disappeared from the lake. The lake trout population stopped reproducing, and the remaining individuals began to slowly starve, as most of its food had disappeared from the lake.

Research is shedding considerable light on how low pH kills trout. The most common cause of death appears to be the disruption of oxygen in the bloodstream. Recall that as water flows over the organism's gill membranes, oxygen is extracted, and the oxygen-enriched blood is transported to the fish's circulatory system. In a highly acidified environment, excessive mucus develops over the gills, essentially causing suffocation. As acid precipitation falls upon the watershed, certain metals are leached from the soils. In particular, aluminum has been shown to interfere with the transfer of oxygen across the gill membranes. Another mechanism is the disruption of the salt balance, especially the concentration of sodium ions, of the fish. No longer in osmotic balance with its environment, the fish experience kidney failure and ultimately death.

Acidic environments also have a negative impact on the life cycle of the trout. In particular, prolonged exposure to pH values lower than 5.0 has resulted in a decrease in the number of eggs deposited in the redd, decrease in the percentage that hatch, and reduction in the growth rates of the fry. Since rainbow trout spawn in the spring, they are particularly susceptible to a condition known as "acid shock." When snow melts, the acidic elements that were locked up during the winter may cause the pH to drop relatively rapidly to lethal levels. The newly hatched fry are most susceptible to succumbing to this condition.

The effects of acid deposition also extend to terrestrial ecosystems that, once degraded, may indirectly have an impact on the aquatic environment. Research has shown that mountaintops may be more acidic than mountain bases, because these high altitude sites are often shrouded in acid-laden clouds. Conifers, mountain laurels, and rhododendrons, which dominate high-altitude forests, are particularly acid-sensitive. Prolonged exposure to this acidic solution results in loss of this vegetative cover and subsequent rise in water temperatures. Small first-order streams are particularly dependent upon vegetative shading to maintain a stable temperature for trout.

With many streams and lakes suffering the effects of acid precipitation, one remedial approach has been liming. The main idea is to replace the lost buffering capacity in the stream by adding limestone. In most cases, limestone is used because it is a naturally occurring material that dissolves slowly, yielding a relatively long-lasting treatment. The limestone is dissolved by the same kind of weathering processes occurring naturally in calcareous soils. In this way the acidity of the water decreases. But there is more to liming a stream than simply dumping the granulated material into water. Studies performed on a number of acidified streams in Virginia showed that particle size of the crushed limestone was a critical factor. The current would wash small-sized particles away too quickly, not allowing time to neutralize the acid. In contrast, large particles (gravel size) would not be moved by the current and thus became incorporated into the stream environment. Sand-sized particles, because of their relatively high surface-area-to-volume ratio, allow for maximum exposure of the particles to the water. When placed in the stream, these particles will be carried approximately 700 to 1,000 feet downstream, settling in pockets along the streambed.

Is liming effective enough in restoring an aquatic system? The answer to that question is not without some ambiguity. Studies have shown that streams and lakes respond positively from a chemical perspective in that the pH and acid-neutralizing capacity increases. While some evidence supports full recovery of the aquatic biota within a three- to five-year time frame, a study of a number of Welsh streams showed that the initial recovery of acid-sensitive invertebrates after liming was not sustained. Even the most positively responsive cases experienced a decline in biota after about five to seven years, necessitating additional liming.

Another impact of an industrialized society on the salmonids probably can be traced to that old phrase, "Better living through chemistry." In particular, during the twentieth century there was a proliferation of organochlorine compounds—synthetic compounds that do not occur in nature but have been put together by chemists from simpler substances. While pesticides have played a major role in agriculture—eradicating harmful insects, controlling the growth of various fungi, and destroying unwanted vegetation—they have proven to be dangerous to trout. Specifically, these chemicals have been linked to declines in trout populations because of their high toxicity. Organochlorine compounds are hydrophobic in that they do not dissolve in water. Instead, the chemical accumulates in the fatty issue of the fish, where the concentration increases with time over the life span of the fish. Tissue samples from trout in Lake Ontario yielded DDT (insecticide) concentrations that were sixteen times higher for a nine-year-old trout compared to a two-year-old trout.

Many of these chemicals enter the top-level organisms through the food chain. In Lake Ontario, background DDT concentrations were on the order of 0.3 to 0.6 parts per thousand (ppt), but trout had concentrations one million times greater than that of the water. This occurs as a result of biomagnification—the increase in pesticide concentration at each successive level of the food chain. For example, if a pesticide is present in only minute amounts in the water, it can be absorbed by plants, which are, in turn, eaten by insects and minnows. These organisms become contaminated, and the concentration of the pesticide increases. When game fish, like trout, repeatedly consume contaminated food items, the level of pesticides in their body fat increases dramatically.

While not all pesticide poisonings reach levels to be lethal to the animals, "sub-lethal" doses can severely impact the life history of the organisms. Fish in streams flowing through farmlands or orchards may repeatedly receive low doses of pesticides as a result of runoff events. Repeated exposures to these pesticides can result in reduced egg production and hatching, lower tolerance to infection, weight loss, and certain behavioral changes. The net effect is diminished health and survival of the individual and decreased population densities.

Even though the use of DDT has been banned in the United States for decades, the warnings about pesticides of Rachel Carson in her book *Silent Spring* (1962) have essentially gone unheeded. With the use of other insecticides, herbicides, and fungicides, we are creating a witch's brew of toxic substances that are chemically stable and slow to degrade in the environment.

A previous chapter detailed the nature of a eutrophic versus oligotrophic lake. Recall that eutrophic lakes undergo physical, chemical, and biological changes as a result of nutrient inputs. Essentially these changes reflect the natural evolution or aging process of the lake.

In the process of cultural eutrophication, excessive nutrients, mostly nitrates and phosphates, enter the aquatic environment as a result of human activities such as agriculture, urbanization, and discharges from industrial and sewage-treatment plants. The addition of these nutrients can profoundly affect the biological diversity of the aquatic environment. Culturally driven eutrophication was not recognized as a threat to streams and lakes in Europe and North America until the 1950s and 1960s—with a polluted Lake Erie as a classic example. One of the culprits was the significant increase in the use of synthetic fertilizer during this period to improve agricultural yield per acre. When nitrogen-based fertilizer is applied to a field with the specific purpose of increasing crop yield, plants may assimilate less than half of this application for use in the photosynthetic process. As a result of poor agricultural practices, a considerable portion of this fertilizer enters the surface and ground water conduits of the hydrologic cycle. These nutrients are then transported to reservoirs, like lakes and ponds, that essentially trap this influx of nutrients. This, in turn, as we have seen, leads to the following chain of events: plant growth, decay, and oxygen consumption. By subsequently reducing the oxygen concentration, cultural eutrophication has the potential to profoundly alter fish community structure, because tolerance to low oxygen concentrations varies considerably from species to species.

During the 1960s, numerous streams in Sweden were highly eutrophic as a result of poor wastewater treatment. As a consequence, population of oxygen-sensitive species, like the brown trout, disappeared from these streams. During this same period, Lake Erie was "dying." Large mats of rotting green algae covered the beaches and near-shore spawning shoals vital to fish stocks. Decomposition of dead algae in the offshore waters depleted the oxygen in these waters and led to a reduction in the abundance of sensitive aquatic organisms such as mayflies and trout. In a more recent study (1992–95) of the streams of the Central Columbia Plateau, the results were not encouraging in that the level of eutrophication in these streams has increased over this period. This resulted in dissolved oxygen concentrations below the level (5 mg/L) required for many species. Minnows, because of their tolerance to lower water quality, presently dominate streams that once contained rainbow trout.

Though water quality has improved in many areas, little is known about how fish populations have responded to these improvements. One critical factor is the ability of species to recolonize impacted areas. For example, certain salmonids may be able to quickly reclaim the habitat due to their ability to migrate over great distances, pass over obstacles, and live in both fresh- and saltwater environments. Other more sedentary species may be less successful at reclaiming their home waters. One study showed that with improved water quality brown trout increased due to increased oxygen concentrations. Correspondingly, the nine-spined stickleback that had previously inhabited the same water decreased due to increased predation or competition with the trout. Hence, improved water quality will lead not only to recolonization of desired species but will promote biotic interactions that play a larger role in structuring fish communities.

The litany of threats that the salmonids must contend with also includes an infection—whirling disease. A parasite, *Myxobolus cerebalis,* attacks the head and spinal cartilage of juvenile trout and salmon, leading to erratic, tail-chasing (whirling) behavior, feeding difficulties, and increased susceptibility to predators. In severe infections, the disease is responsible for high rates of mortality in fingerling trout. Those trout that survive until the cartilage hardens will have a normal life span but are marred by skeletal deformities.

This parasite originated in Europe but found its way to North America in the 1950s. The disease has spread to twenty-two states, including over seventy stream reaches in Montana and almost all major watersheds in Colorado. It is considered the greatest single threat to the wild trout populations of Montana. Once established in a stream, the disease is impossible to eliminate. There has been success in eradicating the disease in closed impoundments, like lakes, but in moving waters the disease cannot be contained or its impact on aquatic life diminished. It has taken a severe toll on the wild trout population. Though whirling disease can affect nearly all species of salmonids, research has shown that rainbow and cutthroat trout appear to be the most susceptible. Brown trout do become infected with the parasite, but they appear to have immunity to the infection and have not been as greatly affected as other species.

The life cycle of the whirling disease parasite involves two distinct stages and two hosts. The spores from the parasite are released when an infected fish dies. These spores commonly number in the thousands to millions and are very hardy—living in a stream up to thirty years. A common aquatic worm, *Tubifex tubifex,* then consumes the spores. While residing in this host, the spores change into a new stage—*Triactinomyxon.*

In this form the parasite can infect the fish either when the worm releases the parasite or if the fish consumes the worm. Once in the trout, the effects of the disease occur within one and a half months, and in three to four months the parasite produces more spores that will start the cycle again when the fish dies.

What is being done to combat whirling disease? A number of options are being considered, including developing resistant strains of trout, finding a vaccine, containing the disease by stricter regulations regarding the transport of hatchery-raised fish, and raising trout to the age that they are essentially immune from the disease. In particular, Montana scientists have successfully imprinted wild trout eggs with a genetic marker that will program the fry to emerge earlier from the redd, thus avoiding periods of heavy infestation. As researchers from universities and federal and state agencies continue to angle for answers, there is hope for the salmonids from this threat.

What can you do to prevent the spread of the disease? First and foremost, do not transport live fish or fish parts from one watershed to another. If fishing in known infected waters, take extra precaution to clean all equipment thoroughly, including wading boots. Pay particular attention to any mud that may have stuck to the waders and dump any water from those waders. Though live infected fish are the main vectors for the spread of the disease, it is probable anglers could carry the disease on their equipment.

Probably no area has generated more controversy within industrial communities, environmental groups, political organizations, and the society of fly anglers than the impact of dams. The debate has been most vitriolic in the Pacific Northwest, where there is a long history of dam construction. Is it more than just a coincidence that the beginning of the decline in the salmon harvest coincided with the era of dam-building on the Columbia River and its tributaries? The center of the controversy revolves around the use of water for migrating salmon and sea-run trout versus the human benefits derived from hydro-generation of electricity, irrigation, and flood control. From the fish's point of view, the crux of the problem is getting the juveniles down the river to the sea and the adults up the river to their spawning sites. And to get fish either up or down involves particular attributes of the river flow—discharge, velocity, timing, and quality.

Young salmon are biologically programmed to migrate seaward at the time of spring snowmelt. The increase in river strength facilitates the seaward sweep of the smolts. Since dams cause impoundment of water behind them and hence a decrease in discharge, the young salmon have to expend more energy to reach their destination. In addition, if delays occur due to dams, the physiological transformation of the young salmon to live in saltwater is upset. Timing is of utmost importance; the salmon's survival depends upon it! These migrating fish are tuned to environmental "cues" that trigger their movement. Since dams cause unnatural fluctuations in water levels, the juvenile salmon may miss their opportunity to begin their journey. A trip on the Columbia River that once took three weeks is now extended to seven weeks.

It only gets worse for the salmon. Since dam reservoirs alter the thermal characteristics of the previously free-flowing river, solar-heated waters may induce negative physiological changes in the young salmon. Even if the salmon begins its migration, it still has to run the gauntlet of dams stretching across the river. Though measures have been devised to shunt the young salmon around the hydroelectric generating turbines, approximately 50 percent of the juveniles still go through the turbines. In order to reduce turbine-induced mortality, another option has been to physically truck or barge the salmon around the dams. Such efforts have been successful to a limited degree, but significant mortalities still result if the shipping distance involved is relatively long; and the cost is prohibitively high, averaging thirty million dollars per year on the Columbia River alone.

Ocean-returning salmon have the problem of overcoming the physical obstacle imposed by dams. These massive walls of concrete and steel, stretching tens of stories in the air, have altered the natural gradient of the river. In order to address this problem, many dams have been retrofitted to include "fish ladders." Fish ladders consist of a series of concrete steps that allow the athletic salmon to incrementally ascend to the top of the dam. Before the advent of dams, salmon jumped up waterfalls in their upstream migration. Now the jumps are over man-made cataracts. But some don't make the passage—approximately 5 to 10 percent of the adults succumb in attempting to negotiate these barriers. At 5 percent mortality, salmon that have to pass seven dams on the Columbia River have only a 1-in-3 chance in making the complete journey. It is undeniable that dams have been, in part, responsible for the elimination of many native salmon runs in the Pacific Northwest. While there seems to be little hope of eliminating the woes caused by these dams in the near future, some progress is being made on the opposite coast. In a precedent-setting case, an agreement was reached between environmentalists and industrialists to demolish the Edwards Dam on the Kennebec River in Maine. Previously, this obsolete dam located on the lower reach of this river was a major impediment for migrating fish.

As early as the 1860s, Mormons began diverting water from the Snake River watershed for use in irrigating crops. From this auspicious beginning, today more than 7 million acres receive their water supply from irrigation sources in the Pacific Northwest. Is there enough water for both the salmonids and humans to survive? In the relatively dry areas of eastern Washington and Idaho, farmers are reluctant about letting stored water be used for fish. Their economic survival depends on utilizing reservoirs of water for extensive irrigation of farmland. But in this arid environment, irrigation is very inefficient, since a significant amount of the water never reaches the crops. Putting two feet of water on a one-acre potato field requires extracting ten or more acre-feet of water out of the river because of loss from seeping ditches, evaporation, and inefficient farming practices. Of this amount withdrawn for irrigation, only one-third may return to the river, but not in the same condition. The water that reenters the river is often warmer, less oxygenated, saltier, siltier, and contains a potent concoction of pesticides and fertilizers.

Another volatile issue in the Pacific Northwest is that of habitat alteration from logging, agricultural, and grazing practices. Historically, much of the land in the center of the Columbia River basin was dominated by grasslands with an established riparian community, which provided food and shelter, stabilized stream banks, and maintained cool water temperatures. Surveys of this area have shown a drastic decrease in canopy cover (80 percent), substantial bank erosion (70 percent), and higher water temperatures that may partially account for the disappearance of rainbow trout, which were native to this area. Fallen trees, previously bordering a stream, play a vital ecological role in the lives of both juvenile and adult salmon. In natural rivers, the migrating young salmon are often swept out of the river too quickly if there is an absence of fallen trees for them to have temporary respite from the torrent. In addition, the logjams created by these trees facilitate the formation of pools that often provide spawning sites for the fish. To aid the logging industry, the U.S. Forest Service has built 360,000 miles of roads in the national forests—seven times the length of the interstate highway system. These roads cross streams hundreds of thousands of times throughout the national forests. These roads often facilitate the occurrence of mudslides during periods of heavy rainfall, since the covering vegetation has been removed. Silt-clogged rivers have a significantly reduced flow that can result in strangulation of salmon embryo.

With all of the environmental and human gauntlets that a trout has to run in order to survive and flourish in its stream or lake, a number of well-meaning resource managers have long proposed supplementing the natural fish population with raising fish in captivity. These hatcheries start with the best intentions, to greatly increase a depleted fish population by rearing young in safety. But a close examination of their role shows that hatcheries function to make up for—and thereby implicitly condone—the wanton destruction of fish habitat.

Though managers, biologists, or anglers do not universally hold this belief, there can be no doubt about the proliferation of hatcheries in our society. Within the Columbia River basin alone, there are more than eighty hatcheries that have been built to mitigate the anticipated damage resulting from dams and habitat degradation.

How do hatchery-raised fish perform in their new environment? The consensus of scientific opinion is that these fish do not fare well after they are released. Because they are selected from a small subset of fish, hatchery fish are often inbred, sometimes exhibiting physical abnormalities and behavioral problems. Essentially, these fish are not "street smart." Having been raised on a diet of food pellets and generally sheltered from any predators, these newly introduced fish must fend for themselves by seeking both shelter and food.

Research has shown that in some streams concentration of wild trout may be as low as one trout per square yard. Even at this level the trout can severely deplete the available food supply, and subsequently their growth will be stunted. Hatchery fish released into these streams increase the density to as much as five fish per square yard, resulting in starvation for both wild and captive fish.

Of all the trout species, the rainbow trout has been most amenable to being raised in captivity on a relatively large scale. As in nature, the main requirement for successful trout-rearing is an adequate supply of cold, clean water. The amount of necessary water flow will vary depending upon a number of factors: quantity of fish to support, water temperature, and season. A ballpark figure of five hundred gallons per minute will support a modest fish production operation. Water temperature for rearing juvenile trout needs to be between $55°$ and $64°F$, with even colder waters better for trout eggs and fry. But if cold spring water is used in the operation, it should be free of metallic salts, which can be toxic to fish even at minute concentrations.

Though trout can be raised in ponds and tanks, the raceway is the system most commonly used in North America to contain the trout during the growth phase. Raceways are generally narrow concrete channels, 7 to 13 feet in width, with a depth of seldom more than 3 to 4 feet. The channels may have an overall length of up to 300 feet but are screened into several sections, having a common water supply from beginning to end. The name indicates the fact that the water flows quickly through the channel to keep the water oxygenated and to flush out waste products. When the raceway is utilized for trout restocking of streams, these captive fish will have become acclimated to flowing water similar to what it will experience in a natural stream.

The determination of an accurate number of fish, stock assessment, is important with regard to evaluating the overall health of the population and implementing management strategies. Managers cannot make informed decisions about fish creel limits, harvesting size, and length of fishing season without quantifying the population size.

The methods employed to assess population size can be divided into two categories: capture versus noncapture. With regard to the former, a common technique employed by fisheries biologists is electric shocking. Essentially, a particular stream reach is selected, and an electrical current administered to the water. The current immobilizes the fish for a brief period, during which they float to the surface, where they can be counted by the observing team. Efficiency can vary significantly according to a number of different factors, and detailed quantification of large aquatic systems is still debatable. Though the technique is widely employed and methodologies are well established, additional research needs to be carried out to evaluate the long-term effect, if any, of electric shocking on the organism.

With regard to noncapture methods, electronic fish counters have been employed successfully in estimating the number of migratory salmonids in rivers. As the fish navigate upstream, design features in fish passes around the dams allow the fish to be confined for counting. Though the method cannot distinguish between large sea-run trout and salmon, the use of photographic equipment can complement this technique. The use of hydro-acoustics (sonar) has been quite prevalent in the freshwater environment. The technique allows for large spatial sampling but has the disadvantage of not separating individual species. It is more applicable where there are few species occupying the same location. Direct human observation may take the form of actually entering the environment (diving) to assess the population or using remote techniques (cameras) positioned outside the system. This method is obviously time-consuming and laborious, limiting it to small aquatic systems.

Although I may have painted a rather bleak picture with regard to the current state of the salmonid population in U.S. waters, there have been some success stories. In particular, the Cranberry River, which flows along the border of the Monongahela National Forest in West Virginia, was once considered a virtual biological desert with regard to its trout population because of more than two decades of receiving acidic precipitation. But due to a concerted restoration effort, the stream has again become a major fly-fishing destination for East Coast anglers. In these instances, dedicated conservationists, anglers, and simply concerned citizens have played a crucial role in tipping the land-use scales to preservation and reservation.

The origin of the "environmental movement" of today can be traced back more than four decades to the first Earth Day, but the state of the environment was a major theme in the life of Thoreau, who deplored the encroachment of human works on the river. Although there are no simple solutions to the problems with which the salmonids are beset, conservation organizations like Trout Unlimited, the Nature Conservancy, the Federation of Fly Fishers, and Theodore Gordon Fly Fishers are fighting the battle on many fronts, including education and increasing public awareness in this area. In the same vein, it is my hope that you have come away from *The Science of Fly-Fishing* with a richer appreciation and understanding of the fascinating world of fly-fishing.

Sources

Ahrens, C. D. 2000. *Meteorology today: An introduction to weather, climate, and the environment.* Pacific Grove, Calif.: Brooks/Cole.

Aquinas, T. 1924. *Summa contra gentiles.* Ed. English Dominion Friars. London: Burns & Oates.

Aristotle. 1941. *The politics in basic works of Aristotle.* Ed. Richard McKeon. New York: Random House.

Barica, J. 1982. Lake Erie oxygen depletion controversy. *Journal of Great Lakes Research* 8:719–22.

Behnke, R. J. 1972. The systematics of salmonid fishes of recently glaciated lakes. Journal of the Fisheries Research Board of Canada 29:639–71.

————. 2001. American brown trout: An immigration story. *Fish and Fly* 1(3):25–33.

Berner, E., and R. Berner. 1987. *The global water cycle: Geochemistry and environment.* Englewood Cliffs, N.J.: Prentice-Hall.

Berners, Dame J. 1963. Modernized text of the earliest surviving version of the *Treatise in the origins of angling* by John McDonald. Garden City, N.Y.: Doubleday.

Beschta, R., and W. Platts. 1986. Morphological features of small streams: Significance and fluctuation. *Water Resources* 22:369–79.

Bilby, R. E., and G. E. Likens. 1980. Importance of organic debris dams in the structure and function of stream ecosystem. *Ecology* 61:1107–13.

Bisson, P. A., J. L. Nielson, R. A. Palmson, and L. E. Grove. A system of naming habitat types in small streams streamflow. In *Acquisition and utilization of aquatic habitat inventory information,* 62–73. Portland, Oreg.: American Fisheries Society.

Borger, G. 2001. Color vision in trout and salmon. www.finefishing.com/1flyfish/flies/colorvision%20trout.htm.

Briscoe, H. 2001. Observations on fly rod construction: The case for the solid rod. www.hexagraph.com.

Browning, M. 1998. *Haunted by waters: Fly fishing in North American literature.* Athens: Ohio University Press.

Campbell, A. 2001. Graphite rod building: How rod blanks are made makes a difference. www.flyanglesonline.com/begin/graphite/part2.html.

Camuto, C. 1988. Consciousness of streams. *Sierra* (March/April): 48–51.

Caro, T. M., and M. K. Laurenson. 1994. Ecological and genetic factors in conservation: A cautionary tale. *Science* 263:485–86.

Carson, R. 1962. *Silent spring.* Boston: Houghton Mifflin.

Caucci, A., and B. Nastasi. 1986. *Hatches II: A complete guide to fishing the hatches of North American trout streams.* New York: Lyons & Burford.

Cronan, C. S., and C. L. Schofield. 1979. Aluminum leaching in response to acid precipitation: Effects on high elevation watersheds in the northeast. *Science* 204:304–6.

Cole, J. 1989. *Fishing came first.* New York: Lyons & Burford.

Cummins, K. 1974. Structure and function of stream ecosystems. *BioScience* 24:631–41.

Des Jardins, J. R. 1997. *Environmental Ethics: An introduction to environmental philosophy.* Belmont, Calif.: Wadsworth.

Dickson, D. 1998. Fly fishing Pacific salmon in fresh water. www.flyfishsteelhead.com/stories/ffsalmon.htm.

Dingman, S. L. 1994. *Physical hydrology.* New York: Macmillan.

Downey, D. 2000. *St. Marys wilderness liming project.* www.csm.jmu .edu/st.marys/index.html.

Dunfield, R. W. 1985. *The Atlantic salmon in the history of North America.* Ottawa: Department of Fisheries and Oceans.

Elliott, J. M. 1991. Tolerance and resistance to thermal stress in juvenile Atlantic salmon, *Salmo salar. Freshwater Biology,* 25:61–70.

Elliot, R. 1997. *Faking nature: The ethics of environmental restoration.* London: Routledge.

Fletcher, G. L., and R. T. Haedrich. 1987. Rheological properties of rainbow trout blood. *Canadian Journal of Zoology* 65:879–83.

Frissell, C. A., W. J. Liss, C. E. Warren, and M. D. Hurley. A hierarchical framework for stream classification: Viewing streams in a watershed context. *Environmental Management* 10:199–214.

Frohlich, G., and J. Johansson. 1988. Fly-fishing. In *The complete book of sportfishing,* ed. Göran Cederberg. New York: Bonanza.

Gierach, J. 1990. *Sex, death and fly-fishing.* New York: Fireside.

Greenhalgh, M. 1997. *Lake, loch and reservoir trout fishing.* London: Mitchell Beasley.

Haig-Brown, R. 1975. *Fishermen's spring.* New York: Nick Lyons.

Halford, F. 1886. *Floating flies and how to dress them.* Reprint, Moretonhampstead, England: Fly Fisher's Classic Library.

Hamilton, J. R. 1998. Political economy of Pacific Northwest salmon. *Electronic Green Journal* 9: http://egj.lib.unidaho.edu.

Hammond, B. 1994. *Halcyon days: The nature of trout fishing and fishermen.* Camden, Maine: Ragged Mountain.

Hankin, D., and G. Reeves. 1988. Estimation of total fish abundance and total habitat area in small streams based on visual estimation methods. *Canadian Journal of Fish and Aquatic Sciences* 45:834–44.

Hardy, C. 1855. *Sporting adventures in the New World.* London: Hurst & Blackett.

Hemingway, E. 1951. *The old man and the sea.* New York: Scribner.

Herd, A. 2001. *History of fly fishing.* Shropshire, England: Medlar.

Hoar, W. S., and D. J. Randall. 1978. *Fish Physiology.* Vol. 8, *Locomotion.* New York: Academic Press.

Hoover, H. 1963. *Fishing for fun and to wash your soul.* Ed. William Nichols. New York: Random House.

Horwitz, R. J. 1978. Temporal variability patterns and the distributional patterns of stream fishes. *Ecological Monographs* 48:307–21.

Hunter, C. J. 1991. *Better trout habitat: A guide to stream restoration and management.* Washington, D.C.: Island Press.

Hughes, D. 1988. *Reading the water: A fly fisher's handbook for finding trout in all types of water.* Mechanicsburg, Pa.: Stackpole.

———. 1991. *Strategies for stillwater.* Mechanicsburg, Pa.: Stackpole.

Hynes, H. B. 1970. *The ecology of running waters.* Toronto: University of Toronto Press.

Iven, T. C. 1952. *Stillwater flyfishing.* Reprint, Moretonhampstead, England: Fly Fisher's Classic Library.

Jaworowski, E. 1992. *The cast.* Mechanicsburg, Pa.: Stackpole.

Jennings, C. 1935. *A book of trout flies.* Reprint, Moretonhampstead, England: Fly Fisher's Classic Library.

Johnson, P. 1986. Learning the language of a stream. *National Wildlife* (Aug./Sept.):30–35.

Karas, N. 1997. *Brook trout.* New York: Lyons & Burford.

Kondolf, G. M., and M. G. Wolman. 1993. The sizes of salmonid spawning gravels. *Water Resources Research* 29:2275–85.

Kreh, L. 1991. *Longer fly casts.* New York: Lyons & Burford.

Lanman, C. 1848. *A fly casting angler in Canada, Nova Scotia and the United States.* London: Richard Bently.

Lawrence, L. 1992. *Prowling Papa's waters: A Hemingway odyssey.* Atlanta: Longstreet.

Leeson, T. 1994. *The habit of rivers: Reflections of trout streams and fly fishing.* New York: Lyons & Burford.

Leopold, L., and W. Langbein. 1966. River meanders. *Scientific American* 214:60–70.

Leopold, L., M. Wolman, and T. Miller. 1964. *Fluvial processes in geomorphology.* San Francisco: W. H. Freeman.

Levin, P., and M. Schiewe. 2001. Preserving salmon biodiversity. *American Scientist* 89:220–27.

Levinton, J. 2001. *Marine biology: Function, biodiversity, ecology.* New York: Oxford University Press.

Lichatowich, J. 1999. *Salmon without rivers: A history of the Pacific salmon crisis.* Washington, D.C.: Island Press.

Likens, G. E. 1972. Eutrophication and aquatic ecosystems. In *Nutrients and Eutrophication,* ed. G. E. Likens, 3–13. San Diego: American Society of Limnology and Oceanography Special Symposium.

Lingard, S. 1987. Notes on the aerodynamics of a flyline. *American Journal of Physics* 56:756–57

Lopez, B. 1989. *Crossing open ground.* New York: Vantage.

Luscombe, B. 1998. *Fly fishing column.* www.flyfishingbc.com.

Lyman, J. 1999. Cultural values and change. *Virginia Marine Resources Bulletin* 32(3):2–10.

Lyons, N. 1977. *Bright river.* Philadelphia: Lippincott.

———. 1989. *Confessions a fly fishing addict.* New York: Simon & Schuster.

Maclean, N. 1976. *A river runs through it and other stories.* Chicago: University of Chicago Press.

Macke, G. L., S. Hincks, and D. Barker. 2000. *Introduction to aquatic environments.* Course manual. Guelph, Canada: University of Guelph.

Mann, R. H., J. H. Blackbum, and W. R. Beaumont. 1989. The ecology of brown trout *Salmo trutta* in English chalk streams. *Freshwater Biology* 21:57–70.

Marino, V. 1976. *In the Ring of the Rise.* New York: Lyons.

McDonald, J. 1954. *Origins of angling.* New York: Doubleday.

McGowan, C. 1999. *A practical guide to vertebrate mechanics.* Cambridge: Cambridge University Press.

Mobley, C. D. 1994. *Light and water: Radiative transfer in natural waters.* New York: Academic Press.

Monaghan, P. 2002. Scientists fish for solutions to a mysterious killer. *The Chronicle of Higher Education* (Jan. 18): A15–16.

Mosser, E., and W. Buchman. 1980. The dynamics of a flycast. *The Flyfisher* (Fall): 5–9.

Netboy, A. 1974. *The salmon, their fight for survival.* Boston: Houghton-Mifflin.

Newman, R. 2001. The extraordinary rainbow trout. www.bcadventure.com.

Perry, B. 1927. *Pools and ripples: Fishing essays.* Boston: Little-Brown.

Phillips, D. 1996. A basic guide to saltwater fly-fishing in southwest Florida: Fly rod. www.marcos-island-florida.com.

Pobst, D. 1996. *Trout stream insects: An Orvis stream guide.* New York: Lyons & Burford.

Poff, N. L., and J. D. Allan. 1995. Functional organization of stream fish assemblages in relation to hydrologic variability. *Ecology* 76:606–27.

Power, G. 1969. *The salmon of Ungava Bay.* Technical Paper No. 22. Montreal: Arctic Institute of North America.

Pulman, G. 1841. *Vade mecum of fly fishing for trout.* Axminster: E. Willis.

Quinnett, P. 1994. Pavlov's trout. *American Forests* 86:44–47.

Raines, H. 1994: *Fly fishing through midlife crisis.* New York: William Morrow.

Raleigh, R., L. Zuckerman, and P. Nelson. 1986. *Habitat suitability index models and instream flow suitability curves: Brown trout.* Washington, D.C.: U.S. Fish and Wildlife Service Biol. Report No. 82.

Randall, D. J., and C. Daxboeck. 1984. Oxygen and carbon dioxide transfer across fish gills. In *Fish physiology,* ed. W. Hoar and D. J. Randall. New York: Academic.

Raymond, S. 1995. *The year of the trout.* Seattle: Sasquatch.

Richards, C. 1989. The practical entomologist. In *Sports Afield: Treasury of fly-fishing,* ed. T. Paugh, 35–39. New York: Lyons and Burford.

Robson, J. M. 1990. The physics of fly casting. *American Journal of Physics* 58:234–44.

Ronalds, A. 1990. *Fly fisher's entomology.* Secaucus: Wellfleet.

Roosevelt, T., 1990. *Outdoor pastimes of an American hunter.* Harrisburg, Pa.: Stackpole.

Rosenbauer, T. 1984. *The Orvis fly-fishing guide.* New York: Lyons & Burford.

Russel, A. 1864. *The salmon.* Edinburgh: Edmonston & Douglas.

Safina, C. 1996. *Song for the blue ocean.* New York: Henry Holt.

Schlosser, I. J. 1982. Fish community structure and function along two habitat gradients in a headwater stream. *Ecological Monographs* 52:395–414.

Schofield, C. L. 1976. Acid precipitation: Effects on fish. *Ambio* 5:228–30.

Schullery, D. 1987. *American fly fishing: A history.* New York: Lyons.

———. 1999. *Royal coachman: The lore and legends of fly-fishing.* New York: Simon & Schuster.

Schwiebert, E. 1955. *Matching the hatch.* New York: Winchester.

Skues, G. 1939. *Nymph fishing for chalkstream trout.* Reprint, Moretonhampstead, England: Fly Fisher's Classic Library.

Smith, J. A. 1996: Catastrophic rainfall from an upslope thunderstorm in the central Appalachians: The Rapidan storm of June 27, 1995. *Water Resources Research* 32:3099–133.

Spolek, G. 1986. The mechanics of fly casting. *American Journal of Physics* 54:832–35.

———. 1987. Where the action is. *American Fly Fisher* 13(4):7–12.

———. 1988. Where the action is: Part 2. *American Fly Fisher* 14:2–9.

Swisher, D., and C. Richards. 1971. *Fly fishing strategy.* New York: Crown.

Taylor, P. 1986. *Respect for nature.* Princeton, N.J.: Princeton University Press.

Thoreau, H. D. 1997a. *Walden. The Portable Thoreau.* Ed. Carl Bode. New York: Penguin.

———. 1997b. A week on the Concord and Merrimack Rivers. In *The Portable Thoreau,* ed. Carl Bode. New York: Penguin.

Tirana, T. 1996. *Fly fishing: A life in mid-stream.* New York: Kensington.

Venables, R. 1662. The experienced angler. In *The Atlantic salmon in the history of North America* by R. W. Dunfield, 4. Ottawa: Department of Fisheries and Oceans.

Vogel, S. 1992. Copying nature: A biologist's cautionary comments. *Biomaterials* 106:63–79.

———. 1994. *Life in moving fluids.* Princeton, N.J.: Princeton University Press.

VonKienbusch, C. 1958. *Introduction to the the art of angling.* Princeton, N.J.: Princeton University Press.

Walton, I. 1975. *The compleat angler.* New York: Weather Vane.

Ward, J. V. 1989. A mountain river. In *The rivers handbook,* ed. P. Calow and G. Petts, 493–510. Oxford, U.K.: Blackwell Scientific Publications.

Webster, J. R., and B. C. Patten. 1979. Effects of watershed perturbation on stream potassium and calcium dynamics. *Ecological Monographs* 49:51–72.

Webb, P. W. 1991. Comparison of the mechanics of routine swimming of rainbow trout. *Canadian Journal of Fisheries and Aquatic Sciences* 48:583–89.

Wohl, E. 2000. *Mountain rivers.* Washington, D.C.: American Geophysical Union.

Index

acceleration, 33; role in casting, 40–41

acid rain, 175–76; effect on trout, 178–79; influence of bedrock on, 176–77; tolerance of aquatic life to, 177–78

acid shock, 178

Adirondack Mountains, susceptibility to acidification, 177

Aeliannus, Claudius, 2

aging of lakes, 125

air resistance, 38, 43, 46–47, 50

algae, 73, 76, 131, 178

American Fishing Tackle Manufacturers Association: line classification system, 21

anadromous, salmon as, 101

angle, origin of meaning of term, 1

anoxic conditions in lakes, 123

Appalachian Mountains, as acidsensitive region, 177

Aquinas, Thomas, 6

Arctic char, life cycle, 169–71

Aristotle, 6

aspect ratio, 96–98

Atlantic salmon: alevin, 165; grisle, 166; kelts, 165; parr, 165; racers, 165; smolts, 166

attractors, 15

Baetis, 112

Battenkill River, as trout stream, 59

Behnke, Ralph, 163

Berners, Dame Juliana, 3, 12

Bernoulli's principle, 90–91, 99

biological production: allochthonous, 77; autochthonous, 76–77

blue haze, 138

body form of fishes: attenuated, 93; compressed, 93; depressed, 93; fusiform, 93

Borger, Gary, 144

brook trout: life cycle and characteristics, 158–61

Browning, Mark, 1, 9–10, 15

brown trout: fishing for, 163; life cycle and characteristics, 162–64

Buchman, William, 40, 51

buckling, 31

buffering, 179

bull trout, spawning requirements of, 170

caddisflies: identification, 108–9; life cycle, 109–11

Camuto, Christopher, 59

carotenoids, 126

Carson, Rachel, 181

casts: backward, 39; curve, 49–50; forward, 40–41; roll, 48–49

catch and release, 14, 172–73

Cayley, Sir George, 94

Chaoborus, 118

char, 158–59

chlorophyll, 140

Cleopatra, 2

Trout Unlimited, 12, 104, 190
tubular rod, 30; resisting bending
  loads, 30–32
two-story fishery, 124

ultraviolet rays, 138–39

visible light, 135
vision in fish, 141–43; field of
  vision, 151–52

wading in streams, 90–92
Walton, Izaak, 1, 3–4, 12
watershed, 57; drainage basin, 57;
  drainage divide, 57
weight, physics perspective on, 37

whirling disease, 183–84; com-
  bating, 184; effect on trout,
  183; *Myxobolus cerebalis,* 183;
  Triactinomyxon, 183–84; *Tubifex
  tubifex,* 183
wilderness, contrasting views on, 7
windrows, 128
winterkill, 123–24
Wohl, Ellen, 73
wood debris, 70
work, physics perspective on,
  36–37
Wulff, Lee, 11

zooplankton, 127, 131–32